sheeple

sheeple

CAUCUS CONFIDENTIAL
IN STEPHEN HARPER'S OTTAWA

Garth Turner

KEY PORTER BOOKS

Library and Archives Canada Cataloguing in Publication

Turner, Garth
  Sheeple: caucus confidential in Stephen Harper's Ottawa / Garth Turner.

ISBN 978-1-55470-179-7

  1. Turner, Garth. 2. Politicians—Canada—Biography.
3. Internet—Political aspects—Canada. 4. Blogs—Political
aspects—Canada. 5. Internet in political campaigns—Canada.
6. Canada—Politics and government—2006-. I. Title.
FC641.T87A3 2009   971.07'3092   C2008-906635-9

THE CANADA COUNCIL | LE CONSEIL DES ARTS
FOR THE ARTS | DU CANADA
SINCE 1957 | DEPUIS 1957

ONTARIO ARTS COUNCIL
CONSEIL DES ARTS DE L'ONTARIO

The publisher gratefully acknowledges the support of the Canada Council for the Arts and
the Ontario Arts Council for its publishing program. We acknowledge the support of the
Government of Ontario through the Ontario Media Development Corporation's Ontario
Book Initiative.

We acknowledge the financial support of the Government of Canada through the Book Publishing Industry Development Program (BPIDP) for our publishing activities.

Key Porter Books Limited
Six Adelaide Street East, Tenth Floor
Toronto, Ontario
Canada M5C 1H6

www.keyporter.com

Text design and electronic formatting: Alison Carr
Printed and bound in Canada

09 10 11 12 13 5 4 3 2 1

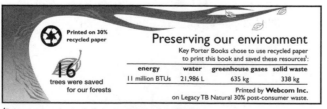

Printed on 30%
recycled paper

Preserving our environment

Key Porter Books chose to use recycled paper
to print this book and saved these resources[1]:

energy	water	greenhouse gases	solid waste
11 million BTUs	21,986 L	635 kg	338 kg

46
trees were saved
for our forests

Printed by **Webcom Inc.**
on Legacy TB Natural 30% post-consumer waste.

[1]Estimates were made using the Environmental Defense Paper Calculator.

FSC

Mixed Sources
Product group from well-managed
forests, controlled sources and
recycled wood or fiber
Cert no. SW-COC-002358
www.fsc.org
© 1996 Forest Stewardship Council

Contents

Dooced
To lose one's job because of a website.

Blog
From "web log." A website, usually maintained by an individual, with regular entries of commentary, descriptions of events, or other material such as graphics or video. Entries are commonly displayed in reverse chronological order. "Blog" can also be used as a verb, meaning to maintain or add content to a blog.

CHAPTER ONE

Dooced

NOT LONG AFTER WATCHING MYSELF ON TV being thrown out of my job, I sat and wrote a substantial portion of this book. At the time, I was an independent member of the Canadian House of Commons, formerly a Conservative MP, until the prime minister had enough of me and my lip and my blog.

As a career journalist, I'd been in the habit of making notes about everything. That proved pivotal in this process of recreating the difficult months I spent on the inside of the Conservative caucus of Stephen Harper, as I became the reluctant online bad boy of Canadian politics. This book, then, will take you into the prime minister's Centre Block office, the PMO control centre in the Langevin Block, the national caucus rooms, and other spots that rarely enjoy daylight.

A further portion was written following my decision to join the federal Liberal caucus and work with Stéphane Dion, just weeks after he'd been selected, surprisingly and with ultimately disastrous results, as party leader and was already under attack. As such, I could witness the striking difference between the two leaders, and the reaction of his party to me, who had been ousted for the alleged and highly treasonous crime of not respecting confidentiality. A conservative all my life, former Progressive Conservative MP, national party leadership candidate, and cabinet minister, my immersion into liberalism proved uneven and ironic.

Other sections were done after I became special advisor to the leader of the official opposition and a member of his shadow cabinet, after he'd privately admitted to a mounting crisis of communications and turned to his digital MP for help. "He wants you to be in charge," Dion's principal secretary, Johanne Senecal, told me one winter afternoon in early 2008. The veteran Liberal strategist and top OLO official looked more serious than usual as she sat behind her oversized antique desk. There was a serious whiff of disbelief in the air.

The following morning, as the only elected politician at the long, glass-topped table in the leader's substantial boardroom next door, I joined the inner circle, which dealt daily with problems engulfing the party and the leader. Soon I took over formal briefings of my caucus colleagues, then helped plan and launch one of the biggest gambles in political history—a carbon tax, at a time of economic meltdown.

Further sections were penned in the weeks following the 2008 federal election, in which my local contest, by way of an all-candidates debate, was described thusly in *Maclean's* magazine by columnist Aaron Wherry:

> In electoral parlance, Halton is a swing riding, one of maybe two dozen in Ontario where a winner isn't obvious and the difference between, say, a Conservative majority and a Liberal minority may well be decided. The two ruling parties have traded Halton for more than a century. Including parts of Burlington, Milton and Oakville, this is a booming stretch of suburbia familiar with both affluence and job losses (Ford's Oakville plant is nearby). In 2006, it went Conservative, by 1,900 votes. Then Halton's MP the aforementioned Mr. Turner, went Liberal, due to irreconcilable differences with Harper's caucus. Harper then appointed Raitt, CEO of the Toronto Port Authority, a coal miner's daughter with three degrees and two kids, to run against him.
>
> Beneath a large wooden cross, the congregation—maybe a

hundred people seated in the pews—seems evenly split. The Tory is bright, well-spoken and passive-aggressive—all nods and shrugs and patronizing smiles. The Liberal, in black beard and dark suit, is blustery and dramatic, an evangelist of sorts.

So this period of writing's been one of extreme contrasts, divided loyalties, and defining events. I was a Harper Conservative, a lone wolf Indie, a Dion Liberal, and a liberal-conservative. From one side of the aisle to the other, I learned the campaign tricks and secret aspirations of both great parties. I watched a leader struggle to be human, and another struggle to be less so.

I saw the nakedly aggressive politics of a party tasting power for the first time, and the shocked disbelief of another too accustomed to success. From a caucus room laced with Ol' Time religion, military discipline, and cowed members, I walked into another rife with division, suspicion, and rebellion. On one side was a leader who exercised complete control and inspired fear even as he dispensed the favours of high office, while on the other was an ambitious yet tentative and oddly stubborn man threatened by the ambition of others.

Sadly absent from caucus rooms were the voices of the people. And I blogged it.

So part of this story's about me, which I am choosing to tell after the passions have quelled. When my job as a Conservative MP disappeared in October 2006, the story made headlines all over the place, as I was the first dooced politician. My return to Ottawa more than a decade after I'd left the last time turned out to be a national car crash. Much bent metal. Many spectators.

My embrace of digital democracy was not shared by hostile colleagues who wanted nothing to do with opening up the secrets of

Parliament to the people who'd sent them there. Worse was my discovery that the party I'd been elected into had become more cult than club, led by a man who viewed me as a destabilizing godless outsider. Within ten months of being elected again, riding back into the nation's capital on a populist mission, it was over.

Stripped of my caucus, my party affiliation, my riding nomination, and my political future, the prime minister left me for dead. The clash between an MP who blogged and webcast and talked to reporters, and a leader who valued none of it, proved fatal; but not for long. In a curious twist, six months later, I'd be sitting in the shadow cabinet of the man Stephen Harper most feared, guiding him forward. And while Stéphane Dion praised me in public as the new communications guru, and gambled on my fealty, in private he harboured concern that several times spilled over into rebuke.

The story, then, is also about leadership.

Under Brian Mulroney, I'd watched a prime minister struggle valiantly and vaingloriously with bigger-than-life crises of his own making—Meech, free trade, and the GST. Under Kim Campbell, whose cabinet I joined, I witnessed the failure of expectations as a singular woman leader was crushed by forces too large to slow. Under Stephen Harper, a Reformer who ingeniously hijacked the Conservative brand, I observed a man the voters believed embodied generational change, but who immersed himself in shopworn partisanship and the politics of the past. In Stéphane Dion, I saw a guy improbably thrust into a reality show, naively and bravely and doggedly determined to be the last one off the island.

This was clear one morning in early June 2008, as Dion faced an inner circle of MPs frustrated and hostile over his failure to bring down the minority Harper government and precipitate an immediate election. In a grandiose East Block conference room, around a massive oval table, with Michael Ignatieff to his immediate right and Bob Rae two seats to his left, Dion played his leadership card.

After hearing more than two-thirds of the people in the room argue passionately and bluntly for an election, Dion said quietly but firmly, "I'm not willing. We will not go now." That should have shut down a discussion he did not want to hear. It didn't. What followed was a direct challenge to his leadership by one of the two men who would be king.

"This is the chance we have," a senior member said, his hand shaking a little with emotion. "Don't be tentative." Dion looked over at him, surprise in his eyes. The antagonist leaned forward. The room tensed. "Seize the moment now," he said. Then, "Leader, life is not a rehearsal."

I watched in astonishment at the unapologetic and uninterrupted assault. Such a challenge to Harper would have been inconceivable, the consequences dire. Dion simply stared back, eyes narrowed, and adjourned the meeting. Was he confident? Or called out?

The Liberal leader survived that meeting, although at least two in the shadow cabinet room ensured that pieces of the conflict were leaked to the *Toronto Star* and the *Globe and Mail*—an insurance policy to be cashed in should the Libs lose the next ill-timed vote and the top guy be judged a fool. It proved to be an astute move. In opposition, I learned, knives are never quite sheathed. Caucus discipline is never assured. Leaders are never quite in control. Democracy and mob rule are never suppressed. Nothing is predetermined. Nothing is known about what comes next.

I loved it.

In late 2006, Elizabeth May sat in my kitchen, outlining how we might save the country. She'd brought gifts—a book she'd authored on lobbying, autographed, and a Green Party policy manifesto which, as leader, she'd written. She had made the journey from Ottawa to sell me

on joining her party and sharing her leadership. Charming, empathetic, mothering, May opened a process shortly after my ouster from
the Conservative caucus, which would end sharply in the boardroom
of an Ottawa condo building four months later.

It was obvious she knew the political potency of the Internet.
Completely devoid of a national organizational network, no agents,
no recruiters, no seasoned operatives, and living off a per-vote stipend
from the federal treasury, the Greens had no choice. May understood
that even doubling the popular vote in the next election would see no
party MPs elected (exactly what happened), since no seat is ever won
without concentrating support in a single riding. The need for a high-
profile, blogging, sitting member of the House of Commons was
evident. And, for better or worse, there was only one.

The following weeks brought several insights, as one of my friends
and supporters became her pollster and advisor. The Greens were a
movement, not an organization. The potential for success was huge as
a none-of-the-above alternative in a jaded, cynical time. But Elizabeth
May, for all her understanding of the populist digital potential of her
cause, proved to be a most traditional politician.

Infatuated and attracted by her media image, she became over-
exposed and then challenged by her own statements. May obsessed
about being a part of the televised leaders' debate in the next election,
lobbied leading journalists like the CBC's Keith Boag for it, and made
that, rather than electoral success, her single goal. "Just imagine a
woman up there with all those suits," she whispered, smiling seduc-
tively and squeezing my arm. Then she sweet-talked Dion into an
alliance to enhance her chances of being elected in the Nova Scotia
riding of Conservative minister Peter MacKay by eliminating a Liberal candidate. The backroom deal, steadfastly opposed by senior
advisors to both leaders, stood in stark contrast to the democratization
of the net and the inclusiveness of her cause.

In the end, she did manage to join the four male leaders in the two televised debates, but did not win a seat in Parliament. She also encouraged vote-splitting, which gained her party no power, but did ensure that Stephen Harper would remain prime minister for at least a few years longer.

In 2000, William Stratas and I built a television broadcasting studio inside a truck, hooked it up wirelessly to the Internet, parked it in downtown Toronto, and broadcast live stock market coverage and breaking business news for eight hours a day. In summer the young anchors inside the vehicle parboiled. In winter they asphyxiated on fumes from a kerosene heater. "Like CNN," a Maclean's magazine story on the venture reported, "only cheaper." We aimed to change the nature of media coverage, but were swept away in the tech implosion that preceded 9/11.

Six years later Stratas, as a volunteer, was in the front seat of my truck as we drove to the Justice Building, on the right shoulder of Parliament Hill, for a meeting with House of Commons technical staff. For the first time an MP had asked for a direct data pipeline, to enable necessary bandwidth for a webcasting studio in his office. We aimed to change the nature of political discourse.

In the early days of my return to Parliament, a thirteen-year absence behind me, the events to come were unimaginable. The intervening years had ushered in an information and communications revolution that was transforming all aspects of Canadian life. Online music, online commerce, online blogs, online mail, online shopping—these were the times of eBay, Google, Facebook, and YouTube. It no longer took a truck packed with TV gear and a gaggle of adventuresome sponsors to effect change and help set a public agenda. One person with an interactive blog, a cheap camera, and a robust connection could reach thousands, if not millions. How could this not be the future of politics?

My return to Ottawa was bathed in a belief that the tools had finally arrived to weld together the people and their politicians. The day after the election in January 2006, I blogged this:

> A web-based MP, I'm hoping, can break down some of the walls between voters and politicians, neighbourhoods, and the government, families, and parties. By connecting people intimately with what the federal government does, and letting them access that which it's supposed to offer, maybe we can change the very image of government. No more bronze statues and stone buildings, but a giant shopping mall called Canada, where people go because they actually, seriously want to. Imagine that.

Within a year, the same House of Commons technicians who had hooked me up were disconnecting my data pipeline and piling blue wires on a grey cart. A member of the parliamentary security force stood nearby as I was thrown out of my office.

Two years later, almost to the day, I was no longer in Parliament, in the wake of a general election in which Stephen Harper targeted me for defeat. His weapons included a blizzard of mailers, a forest of election signs, an army of party workers, a phalanx of phone calls, and character assault by political bloggers.

In the days following, I walked the wind-swept beach near my cottage and wondered two things.

Had it been worth enduring the futility and failure of my aborted political career to champion the cause of digital democracy? After all, there's no finality in politics like defeat. An inevitable conclusion seemed to be that voters were simply not ready, interested, or engaged enough to flood through the portal with me. Had my online suicide been utterly without point?

I was also torn over this book. Five days after the election I walked to the edge of my deck with the manuscript in hand and threw it into the lake. A day later, I reprinted it.

I remain unsure of the words that follow, and how they'll be interpreted. This book is not about Stephen Harper, Stéphane Dion, Conservatives or Liberals or me. Rather, its essence is the clash between the old and new ways for democracy to happen in a time of uncertainty, doubt, and fear. Leaders and parties fear the potential of the Internet for the massive destabilization it could bring. In the best of times, it is the online equivalent of an out-of-control town hall meeting. In days like these, maybe a riotous coup.

For individual politicians, a web-based society brings demands for an unachievable level of accountability and openness, wherein every position, belief, public vote, personal action, and past statement becomes the standards against which one's judged. No wonder no other federal elected official in the country followed my lead. No wonder it destroyed me.

And yet, this is the future. Democracy is in immediate need of renewal. In the last Canadian election, in the midst of the worst economic and financial meltdown since the Great Depression, with investments collapsing and panic setting in, almost 40 percent of voters stayed home. Why?

In large part, because of a structure in which people rarely get what they vote for. Our nineteenth-century myth—that representative democracy actually represents anyone.

Citizens have come to know otherwise. Their choice on election day is between political brands and leaders they will never meet, not individuals seeking their support. They know once the results are announced that tracking, influencing, or even contacting their member of Parliament will be virtually impossible. The MP's job has evolved into representing a party to the people, not the people to Parliament. Thus, voting is futile. It only encourages them.

This is the public impotence I sought to change. At every junc-
ture, I was resisted.

On the night of the election in which I lost my seat to a neophyte
Conservative, CTV news reported the prime minister cheered at news
of my defeat. In conventional wisdom, he'd won.

But these are not conventional times.

The story that follows is not a successful one. There's no way to
polish it. I became a polarizing figure in Canadian politics after taking
a key decision in the days following the election of 2006. The prime
minister made a demand I could not accept, and the consequences
followed.

Some people thought I was a heroic figure for choosing the path
I did. Many more believed I was an idiot, or worse, dangerous. Entire
websites were dedicated to my demise and, as an opposition backbencher, I received far more attention from political operatives and
the mainstream media than I deserved. Those people in my riding
who voted for a Conservative and ended up with a Liberal hated my
guts and ultimately were avenged. Those across the nation who supported Stephen Harper, himself a polarizer, piled on.

Not a day passed during my return to Parliament Hill that was
not bathed in controversy and criticism. The contrast with my first
tour of duty as an MP under Mulroney and Campbell was stark. Police
officers watched over my town hall meetings. For more than two years,
I received an average of one threatening email every four hours. But
at the same time, Canadians came to read my words well over a million
times a month—words that were able to carve headlines in dailies a
thousand miles from my laptop.

None of this, the failure nor the influence, would have occurred
without a blog.

The decision to become a web-based MP, to turn my time in
Ottawa into an open discussion board, to poll and engage and reveal,
and to see if digital democracy could improve a system I well knew

was losing relevance, was central to this story. The decision, one would also conclude, was fated. Parties and leaders do not want what a growing legion of citizens ask. A blogger with a foot in both worlds was a dead man walking.

CHAPTER TWO

"We can arrange that. Count on it."

—Ian Brodie, chief of staff, PMO, 2006-2008

JAY HILL SAT IN A STRAIGHT WOODEN CHAIR three feet away. He played with a shirt cuff.

"He came here as sort of a lumberjack," the newspaper bureau chief had told me over lunch at an Italian place on Sparks Street. "Very northern BC, very Reform. But after thirteen years, he's got the corner on Hugo Boss suits now. He seems to sure like it here, but I think he's a bitter man for not making it into cabinet. And he's still a tough guy."

The Honourable Jay Hill, PC MP, now sat waiting for his prime minister to speak. He might not then have been in cabinet (that would come closer in the summer of 2007), but as the newly minted chief government whip, he had been conferred the special and unusual honour of being sworn into the Privy Council, as an afterthought, ten days behind the rest. For the remainder of his life, he would be able to write "Hon." in front of his name. I looked at him for a moment, thinking about the fifteen minutes he had just spent chewing me out in the cabinet committee room down the hall, with the double leather doors to keep words unheard, and wondered what that honour might mean in Fort St. John. I remembered well the couple of times I had stayed there, in the concrete bunker called the Pioneer Hotel, listening to midnight beer bottles being smashed on the sidewalk outside. "Don't forget," the desk clerk had said pointedly when I checked in. "The front doors are locked at 11 p.m. After that, nobody gets in."

Hill straightened the other cuff.

Thirty minutes earlier I sat Dorothy down on a leather couch in the stone corridor on the third floor of Centre Block. To her right was a group of giggly rookie MPs talking nervously, waiting for their audience with the leader. On the left two plainclothes RCMP officers spoke quietly. There were half a dozen more close by at the two entrance points to the passage of power at the top of the staircase descending to the House of Commons. Peter MacKay walked by. The prime minister's executive assistant passed. Hill appeared and did not introduce himself.

"I need to talk to you right now," he said, without noting my wife's presence. Sure, I answered, thinking this might be related to the incident downstairs. He opened a leather door and went through it. I followed, strangely naive.

One floor below, the Art Deco goddess looked down on the Reading Room. Symbolizing the spirit of the printed word and the democratizing spread of information, she stares each week into a space where Conservative members of Parliament meet to caucus behind those leather-clad doors. Tonight the room was emptied of green chairs, a table in the centre piled high with finger foods, around it hungry MPs, many accompanied by overdressed wives from across the country, hesitant in the stone grandeur.

Steven Fletcher wheeled up to me. It was our first conversation. He did not say who he was, but I recognized him from a television feature I'd seen on the first quadriplegic MP—a hugely sympathetic piece showing him campaigning, being carried on a gurney door to door by volunteers. "I just watched Duffy," he said, his attendant standing beside his elaborate chair, "and it was terrible. I'm very disappointed with you. Why are you trying to screw us?" I leaned over to make some points in my own defence, but quickly gave up, since he put the chair in gear. I feared for my toes.

Marjory LeBreton came up, and I brightened. I'd first met her as Brian Mulroney's secretary, the stalwart and faithful and friendly Progressive Conservative, rewarded by The Boss with a seat in the Senate, where she and Hugh Segal and Lowell Murray kept the PC flame alive after 1993 and pilloried the Reform tide that had swept the progressives out to sea. I had not seen Marjory in years. I did not know yet that Stephen Harper had sworn her into his cabinet and made her leader of the government in the Senate. Her vast office down the hall featured floor-to-ceiling carved wooden panels, soaring gothic windows overlooking Parliament's front lawn, a yawning doorway onto the Senate foyer, stone fireplace, and a private, panelled washroom where she hung her favourite Mulroney-era political cartoons, framed in silver, above the Kleenex.

She was all over me. It had only been twelve or fifteen minutes since I did the live hit with CTV in the House of Commons foyer fifty feet away, expressing my disappointment that David Emerson, elected as a Liberal in Vancouver a few days earlier, had been appointed to Harper's cabinet. It was inconsistent, I said, with everything I had heard Conservatives say when Belinda Stronach crossed to the other side. It was not a good start.

Nor was this. LeBreton tore into me, scaring off Michael Chong's young wife, and attracting attention in the crowd. Dorothy was astonished, speechless. "Let's get out of here," I said, turning to her. "I'm supposed to meet Harper in a few minutes anyway."

We headed upstairs.

It quickly became apparent Hill was softening me up for Harper. He sprawled in one of the leather chairs, and I took one opposite. The room was empty, its dozen other chairs placed around the circular cabinet table. Staring down over Hill's shoulder was a Lemieux. A good one.

He started out being collegial, saying he knew what it was like to be a member of Parliament who has strong opinions and the need to express them. I'll never forget, he said, when we had to walk out of the Reform caucus. That was a very difficult time, to take on the leader like that, even when we knew it was the right thing to do.

I listened politely, said nothing, stared at my toes. I'd been a Stephen Harper Conservative MP for a week, and was already seriously regretting it.

During the election campaign Doug Finley, his chief political operative and national campaign director, had disrespected me in a memorable conference call—all over my giving an interview without permission to Jon Chevreau, a *Financial Post* columnist whom I had known for a decade. I thought it an isolated eccentricity, until Finley's twentysomething underlings, Joseph Dow and Jenni Byrne, tried exactly the same in coming days. In fact, in order to get Conservative candidate and future minister Bev Oda to the suburban Toronto studio of CTV instead of me, Byrne had told veteran political broadcaster Mike Duffy I was simply not available. "Don't even get in the car," I was then told. "Oda's already in makeup in Agincourt." I called Duffy, who said they had not even heard she was coming. The knowledge that your party's communications people are, at best, neophytes is not exactly a comfort.

The telltale signs continued after election night, when Harper did not call to congratulate, nor did any of his team. And I remembered that he hadn't called after winning the nomination, either. But at that time I didn't suspect one of the men I defeated in the fierce nomination contest had been backed by a Harper insider and Toronto televangelist and supported by Toronto area MP Peter van Loan. Months later Harper would take van Loan into his cabinet after principled MP Mike Chong quit his post over the PM's hasty move to make the

Quebecois a nation, and later elevate him to the key position as House leader.

(Later, in speaking with other MPs, I confirmed Harper is no Brian Mulroney telephone addict. Whereas Mulroney would call out of the blue, full of effusive praise and leaving his subject—friend and foe alike—swimming in endorphins, Harper does not try to reach out, because in his world view, it's just not required. He is the leader.)

Back upstairs, I studied the Lemieux while Jay Hill yapped on, thinking then about the appointments to Harper's cabinet. Michael Fortier, the unelected advisor and Tory bagman, put into cabinet and justified as such with a Senate appointment. So much for the twin Preston Manning/Reform holy grails of a triple-E Senate, and politicians subject to recall. And David Emerson, elected just a few days before in Vancouver as a Liberal, then shockingly present at Rideau Hall on February 6, smiling and shaking Harper's hand as the new trade minister.

Memories of that day were fresh. As I sat on the empty floor of my new condo in Ottawa that morning, trying to screw together an Ikea entertainment unit, watching the cable guy staple cream-coloured wires into the baseboard, and listening to the news, I was incredulous. And I recalled then, just days after my nomination the May before as the Conservative candidate in Halton, listening on the car radio to news of Belinda Stronach's defection to the Paul Martin Liberals. The impact was the same. Was there no honour left in politics?

The next day the reaction among Conservatives was explosive. It was also sexist, belittling, and—a characteristic I would come to learn was prevalent—morally superior.

Belinda Stronach, we heard, did this because she was an imperfect person. She probably could not help it because she was female ("I think she sort of defined herself as something of a dipstick. An attractive one, but still a dipstick," said Ontario Conservative MPP Bob Runciman). She was without principle ("I said that she whored herself out for power, that's what she did," said Alberta Conservative MLA and Christian fundamentalist minister Tony Abbott). She was cheap ("Some people prostitute themselves for different costs or different prices," said Saskatchewan Conservative MP Maurice Vellacott). And she wasn't too bright ("I've never really noticed complexity to be Belinda's strong point," said Conservative leader Stephen Harper).

In the late spring of 2005, I recalled, Belinda Stronach was worse than a traitor, more dangerous than a spurned lover, her name spat out in Conservative gatherings by Ontario party operatives like Wally Butts and Richard Ciano as one would expel an inhaled bug. The media was at first mesmerized by the Stronach move and its political implications, then repulsed at the misogyny of the reaction. After his initial comments strongly suggesting Belinda was a mental midget, Harper said nothing. He chose not to correct any misconceptions or chastise the boys who had a go at her. She was beneath him.

Eight months later the Rt. Hon. Stephen Harper stared across a few acres of red carpet in the room with the big windows and the gold ceiling, looked a little to his left at Governor General Michaëlle Jean, and then back at the three rows of people waiting to recite their oaths of office. In the front row was David Emerson. Elected fourteen days earlier as a Liberal, after campaigning for the Liberals in Vancouver, and against the Conservatives. Former Liberal cabinet minister. Floor-crosser. Unlike Belinda Stronach, the prime minister told CTV, Minister Emerson was smart. "He is a man of great intelligence, a man with a stellar record in the private sector, who is clearly committed to public service."

The businessman-turned-politician who, two weeks earlier to the day, had said in the Golden Swan restaurant on Vancouver's Victoria Drive that he would like to be "Stephen Harper's worst nightmare," smiled, swore allegiance, and pumped Harper's hand. And nobody once used the word "whore."

✧

Jay Hill was still talking. Telling me about being a grain farmer in northern BC with his brother, and how hard it had been to turn his back on that and get into politics. I asked how big the farm was. Three thousand acres, he said. Hill went into it right out of high school, after being a tree-cutter, then an oil patch greaser, and eighteen years after achieving Grade 12 he was the Reform Party candidate in Prince George-Peace River. He lost that race, but won in 1993, then won twice more, and then decided his leader—Stockwell Day—wasn't good enough to be his leader. On May 15, 2001, Hill and seven other rene-gade former Reformers were suspended from the Canadian Alliance caucus for treason.

But that was different, he was telling me. It was another time. It wasn't easy. Besides, I thought, looking at the big flashy pinky ring Hill always twists when he's stressed, the one he had his parliamentary lapel pin flamboyantly fashioned into, Stockwell Day could not have made him Honourable.

"Why did you do that?" Hill asked. Why, he meant, had I just that day decided my leader might not be good enough.

Ah, why. As if there was a choice. After Emerson and Fortier were made Harper ministers, and the entire cabinet minted, the party called a national caucus. As usual, it took place in the Reading Room, off the Hall of Honour in the Centre Block. I went, of course, but as I walked past the Chateau Laurier in the bitter cold, I was already dreading what was sure to happen.

I was acutely aware that in the riding an avalanche of emails from outraged constituents was flowing, as my political assistant, Esther, watched with her shiny new constituency office phones being over-whelmed by angry callers. Typical is this note I published on my weblog:

I am feeling incredibly betrayed by Stephen Harper.

This is more of the same crap that the Liberals have been serving out for 12 years and which made my blood boil. The lies, the deceit, the arrogance. I couldn't wait to vote those bastards out and vote in some integrity and honesty. But this! This is a betrayal of my confidence in Harper and the Conservative party.

I am a Garth Turner supporter, I pushed for a Conservative win, defended Harper and the Party to friends and relatives, put an "oh-my-God-that's-a-big-election-sign" on my front lawn for the benefit of my neighbours, and railed against the Liberals.

Now? I don't know what or whom to trust in anymore. I am completely disgusted and discouraged. With a single stupid act Harper has extinguished the hope we all had for real change.

You were supposed to be better than this.

At the drugstore checkout in Milton, as I picked up a few things for my trip to Ottawa the night before, dressed in jeans and ski jacket, the cashier and customers in line agreed I must "be trying to keep a low profile, given what's just happened." This was not going well.

I went home and wrote in my blog:

Constituents wonder how I, an avowed democrat who spent months and months knocking on doors to get elected, feel about a cabinet minister who has never even tried to get a vote. And they wonder, after I said any MP who turns coat on their party should have to be re-elected under their new colour, how I now stand on the issue.

Of course, I could take the easy way out. I could tell you that the prime minister never called me to ask my opinion. I could tell you he didn't discuss any issue about the cabinet with me. I could confess that I am not on Harper's speed-dial list—and all that would be quite true. But I am not out to duck anything. I am a

Conservative MP, in times of criticism and controversy, as well as in the times of triumph. That means I also have to accept responsibility.

So, to those who saw these moves as hypocritical and politically crass, I ask two things. First, assume Harper had a plan, knew the risk he was taking, and gambled he was doing the right thing. I have no idea if he did or not. Nor does anyone else. Time will judge this move ruthlessly. Second, help me fight for changes to the system that will put an end to both political treason and unelected politicians. We need legislation to force a by-election when an MP switches parties, forcing him or her to go back to the people for support.

Many of you will know I have two goals: to empower and raise up the position of MP, and to represent the middle class to Parliament. I do the first in the hope that more independent, free-voting, and respected politicians can restore dwindling faith to the whole system. I do the latter because it's time average hard-working families finally got the same attention as special interest groups.

I will try, at first, to get my government to champion these causes. If it does not, I will champion them myself. How will that happen? Well, just watch me. But first, I'm heading up that stone staircase just outside the House of Commons lobby, and past the men who guard the prime minister's office.

Blinded with intentions, I'd stumbled so soon into a morass from which I wouldn't be rescued. Campaigning in poetry, governing in prose, Stephen Harper was not the man I had imagined, nor the one I had portrayed on twenty thousand doubting doorsteps. My first mistake was having misunderstood him. My second, more serious, was saying so.

"Why did you do that?" Hill was asking again. He seemed incredulous, as Fletcher and LeBreton had been. It was as if this was a completely normal development. You know, get elected on a platform of changing the entire political process and creating an open, accountable and transparent government. Then, on the first day, pull a Belinda.

I did not have a good answer this night for Jay Hill, the honourable chief government whip, although at that moment I did not exactly know what he was. A heavy, obviously. Harper's heavy. Acting like a prick, actually. Trying to intimidate me, telling me now that I had a choice to make. Either you're a team player, or you're not, he said ominously. Things can get uncomfortable around here. He paused. You're experienced. You know what I mean.

So I talked to him a bit about my commitment to the voters and to myself, and my desire this time as an MP to avoid compromise and to do the right thing. And he looked at me as a man who had been president of the BC Grain Producers Association and knew all about underlings.

Jay Hill is three years younger than I, born in 1952 in the same small town he lives in now. So I wondered what stress it was in his life that had turned his hair white and etched such lines on his face that, at this moment, were all pointing south. He looked at me in considerable disgust, said we were done, and left the room. I went back to Dorothy in the hallway in time to hear Harper's chief aide call out abruptly to a female staffer. Get to the reception, he said, and come back and tell me if enough people are left for him to go down.

Another woman came out of Harper's corner office and told the giggly MPs to leave, since the prime minister could no longer see them. Then she came over and instructed me to follow her. As I entered, passing the twin guards at the doorway, Hill was now sitting in a straight wooden chair and Harper was three feet away. They both stood up. Hill went for his ring.

✧

Parliament Hill is one of the coldest places on the planet, thanks to a constant north wind that sweeps off the river and keeps the bedsheet-sized flag atop the Peace Tower so exercised it must be replaced every few days. It was minus thirty as I passed through the stone gates, walked past the East Block, and decided to duck through the main doors of Centre Block instead of going the extra two hundred feet to the Members' Entrance. Big mistake.

Through my frosted glasses I could quickly see the blazing lights of the sun guns and the pack of media in front of me. They were camped out in the wide corridor leading to the caucus area. As my lenses cleared, I saw my new colleagues stream by, waving off the horde, hurrying down the hall, running almost, and into the safety of the meeting room. Assuming I was as unimportant as I felt at the moment, I walked past, only to be surrounded.

What do you think of the appointment of Mr. Emerson and Mr. Fortier? I was asked. I have some reservations, I said, and started to move off. Then I heard something unexpected: "But you wrote on your blog there should be legislation to stop floor-crossers. Is that your position?"

Your blog. It stopped me short. "No comment" was suddenly not an option. Politician weasel words would only erase my reason for being in this stone building. Looking back, this was a moment when the written word and the person melded. In becoming a digital MP, whose words were perpetually online, Google-accessible and unretractable, I'd traded off deniability for reach. The blog would bestow perverse power, influence beyond reason, and defence against the country's most powerful man. But it also gave no shelter, nowhere to hide.

"You read my blog?" I asked, staring in the white heat of the scrum lights. And it became obvious in an instant that the dynamics of the moment had changed. It was one thing entirely for a low-profile backbench MP, a Joe Preston or Royal Galipeau or Brian Storseth, to walk by with impunity, having said nothing, written nothing, published nothing. The moment would be forgotten. No clip. They wouldn't be on the news that night. But by writing this blog—which I learned had crossed the firewall between riding and Parliament Hill—I knew I no longer had the luxury. If I contradicted the words there, I'd be a media sellout. If I stood by them, well, a crap storm.

So, the choice was instantly clear. Do what every political instinct in my body was screaming, fudge the answer, muscle my way out of the pack, dismiss my words as an early, unreasoned response, defend the leader, say Mr. Emerson was a damn good choice and run like hell for Room 253-D. Or follow my heart, tell the truth.

"Do you still think floor-crossing is wrong, Mr. Turner?"

Pause.

"Garth?"

I took time to think about this. It seemed like three or four minutes, but was likely a few seconds. I was surrounded on all sides now. Fuzzy grey boom mics dangled over my head and a dozen stick mics brushed up against my beard. Some faces I would come to know very well in the coming months poked through shadows between the blazing white lights. Beatrice Politi, Julie van Dusen, Jane Taber, Bob Fife, Keith Boag. They were all quiet while I thought. For two seconds.

"You criticized Belinda Stronach in the campaign!" "You were against switching parties!" "You wrote about it. How do you defend Emerson?"

So, I said to myself, this is probably it. First caucus. Last rites.

But could it happen so soon? After all, it had been just a few weeks earlier, on the eve of the vote that was to topple the Paul Martin government, November 28, that I'd written this for my future constituents, high that night on the drug of democratic reform, after hours of frigid door-knocking in north Burlington:

So, the hope of our campaign in Halton is that Harper and his media team stress not just the reasons Liberals have to go, but—more importantly—why Conservatives should be given a chance. Do we have a vision and an agenda? Are we more in tune with average voters? Will we provide better, more responsive government? Can we be trusted to spend more wisely, manage more competently, and deal with the issues a majority of people feel are essential? Is there a reason to vote for Conservatives, and not just against Liberals?

If there isn't, we don't deserve to win. But—trust me—that is not going to happen. We are the hope and the future. We have a plan and a pledge. I have walked the streets of this riding, talked with thousands and thousands of people, spent time in their homes, on their driveways, listening to their hopes and frustrations.

At the end of the day, it's pretty simple. People don't want handouts and subsidies, but a level playing field for everyone. Fairness in taxes, honesty in government, a good chance for everyone to get ahead. Leadership is about getting obstacles out of the way, not building them. It's about letting people feel hopeful and optimistic, because they are your partners, not your inferiors.

Esther sent me an email that night after I'd posted my words. "You made me cry," she said. Then the words she always sends me when I surpass her expectations: "You rock." The next day she took a couple of sentences I'd written, blew them up, and posted them on the bulletin board in the campaign office, beside the pro-Harper editorial cartoons clipped out of the collective copy of the meat-eating *Toronto Sun*.

And here I was, ten weeks later. Campaign done. Election won. The MP for Halton—the first Conservative since 1993, after wearing straight through the soles of two pairs of cowboy boots. It has been the longest-fought and hardest-won success in my life, and yet the thin margin of victory on January 23—just under two thousand votes—was a shocking testament to the serious reservations my near-GTA constituents had about the new Conservative party.

The guy I defeated, Liberal Gary Carr, had trouble believing what had just happened to him. After thirteen years of Liberals, and a convincing win in 2004, this was completely unexpected. Two days later one of the local papers published a picture of him standing in a near-deserted campaign office at midnight, staring into his Blackberry, waiting for the final advance poll results to come and rescue him. But I had prevailed—and narrow or not, it was a victory nonetheless. I was going back to Ottawa, an unusual renaissance man, determined in his own mind that this reincarnation would be—above all, even above party—a principled one.

They were still there. The heat of the lights on my face was a stunning contrast to my white-tipped fingers and the drip from my thawing nose. "Do you defend Mr. Harper's cabinet choices?" "Do you stand by what you wrote about floor-crossing MPS?"

And the situation was now clear. How could it be otherwise? Stephen Harper had just done what was good for Stephen Harper, bringing in representation from Vancouver, removing one of the most credible political opponents he would face, giving his neophyte and untested cabinet desperately needed experience, and sticking a fork in Belinda's forehead. But, in doing so, he'd shown early on he had no intention of doing what I'd told electors, of "letting people feel hopeful and optimistic, because they are your partners, not your inferiors."

Suddenly my voters were not his partners, but his victims, and certainly his inferiors. What was wrong in opposition was right in power. The end, Mr. Harper was telling us, justified the means. Suddenly Canada's new government was sounding, well, old.

Looking up a little, I made my decision.

A hundred times thus far, since getting back into politics in May 2005, I had said I was the kind of guy who should be an MP. Had a bunch of careers. Made my money. Been a cabinet minister and a leadership contender. Delivered the big speech. At fifty-seven years of age, I was not looking to forge a political path to the top, or to impress any collection of mentors with my untapped potential. Had enough experience to know the game, and not so much ambition to forget the rules. Never did expect to be named to Harper's cabinet, and any niggling illusions were dashed during the campaign with the back of Doug Finley's hand. Man, no doubts there.

We'd just spent nine months campaigning every day, knocking on twenty-five thousand doors in a riding that had voted Liberal in five elections. This was no triumphant return to public life, but a bottom-up and humbling exercise in political survival.

Being a member of Parliament in the past had been truly enjoyable, despite my youthful aggression. I was looking forward now to returning to Parliament with an array of new experience, new perspective, and the luxury of knowing my circumstances would always allow me to avoid compromise. I also went in a new time of new tools of communication, wedded to blogging and the relentless transparency it demanded.

And here it was, a few days into the job. Not asked to compromise—but expected to compromise, as a certitude, a given, an absolutely expected response to a situation I did not create or influence. And while it could not be known at the time, it was one in which Stephen Harper would place every member of his caucus over and over and over again in the year to come. He is the leader.

So, measuring my words, I answered, "Mr. Emerson is probably the best man for the job. I am sure he'll do well for Canada. But he should get elected as a Conservative first. That's my position, and I'm sticking with it."

I broke off and made my way down the hall towards a clutch of

Conservative MPs who had stood in the shadows to watch, then walked away as I approached.

I was so fucked.

The media was the message, as Conservative MPs gathered for the first time after the January 23, 2006, election. There were 124 of us. The numbers in the caucus room, however, were swelled by the addition of Conservative senators, like Hugh Segal—who within months would quietly distance himself from the Harper fold, apparently disillusioned—and a surprising number of PMO staffers. Ian Brodie. Doug Finley. Ray Novak. Sandra Buckler. William Stairs. Caucus, in my previous experience, had been restricted to elected members.

The old Alliance superstars circulated knowingly—Stockwell Day, Monte Solberg, Chuck Strahl, Jason Kenney. Mixed in were the few Progressive Conservatives who still mattered, namely Peter MacKay and Loyola Hearn. The newly elected Mike Harris squad was prominent: Jim Flaherty, Tony Clement, and John Baird, the latter strutting like a man whose coming cabinet appointment had been more than assured. Trying to figure out who mattered and what to say, and to who, were the newbies, a crop of neo-Cons elected largely in rural areas of the country, since the Harperites had just been, dangerously, shut out of Montreal, Toronto, and Vancouver. And then there was a backbench contingent who, with the exception of old PCers like Nova Scotia's Bill Casey, Calgary's Lee Richardson, Quebec's Jean-Pierre Blackburn, and me, from Halton, was solidly from the Reform days. As it turned out in the months to come—but unknown to me at that moment—these would be the soldiers whose task it was to take me out. And they did the job well.

First caucuses are rarely about anything. They're a time for celebrating joint accomplishments, aggrandizing the campaign just past, lionizing the leader, demonizing the opposition, and talking in the most general terms possible about the months to come. At this caucus everyone in the room was acutely aware that roughly half of them would end up with a cabinet posting or a parliamentary secretary position. Others would be caucus officers—chairs or vice-chairs, deputy whips, and the like. The positions would bring titles, better offices, more pay, and, in the case of ministers, additional personal staff, increased office budgets, cars and drivers, instant media profile, and often departments with budgets in the billions, workforces in the thousands, and the capacity to affect the lives of millions of people.

Most importantly, though, the structuring of this swirling room of people into government strata would signal where in the pecking order Stephen Harper—in a short moment to be introduced as Prime Minister Stephen Harper to unbridled cheers and open doors, as the Parliamentary Press Gallery was uncharacteristically allowed to swarm in—saw them. And his eyes were everywhere.

There were no illusions about where I fit in, even within a few days of the local victory party at the Ramada Inn at the junction of Highways 401 and 25 in Milton, with the well-weathered rock band I'd hired. I had yet to meet Doug Finley, but it was obvious from Harper's coolness towards me at a few campaign events that a serious problem existed. I'd tried hard to understand that. Yes, there was the Chevreau incident, and then the strange Duffy event. In addition, one of Finley's underlings had called one night and ordered me to remove a photo of Harper and Paul Martin sitting, waiting for the first leaders' debate to commence, from my blog. That was it—and I had even, painfully, acquiesced.

I'd used considerable personal capital calling Chevreau and getting him to read me his column before it was published—on an interpretation of Harper's hastily announced capital gains tax break—just to

ensure no national policy incident was created. It was a huge conces-
sion for him to have done that. I'd spoken to Duffy, telling him it was
better for both of us just to be misled by the campaign, at least this
once. Take Bev Oda, I said, even when he told me she was "lousy TV."
And I knocked down the photo—as tame as it seemed—of the two leaders sharing a bench, backs almost touching, staring off in opposite direc-
tions. For some reason, that had made the Harper guys go ballistic.

From where I sat as a candidate, the Conservative campaign was
controlling, manipulative, deceitful, and it viewed the media as a
resource to be used up and thrown away. After spending a career in the
communications business as a newspaper writer, editor, columnist,
and publisher, and as a TV reporter, commentator, anchor, as well as
founder and president of a television production house that created
news and entertainment shows seen on five networks, it was bizarre
to me that twentysomething backroomers were calling the shots and
barking at me, as well as the media veterans.

At first I was sure it was a youthful mistake, but a few weeks into
the Harper road trip, it was clear this was standard procedure. Reporters
were spoon-fed messages each day. Exposure to the leader was scripted
and staged. Most candidates were kept out of sight, or at least out of
microphone range. One, famously, was hidden in a kitchen rather than
be made available for an interview. And internally, journalists were
talked about in the most disparaging terms imaginable, with the
assumption made they could routinely and easily be tricked, controlled, and corralled.

In large part, of course, that's exactly what happened. The media
mistakes that Harper perceived had kept him in opposition following
the 2004 campaign were largely avoided. The Conservative campaign
was judged to be professional and gaffe-free, and the public appetite
for change from Mr. Dithers and the residue of the Liberal sponsorship
scandal was undiminished by news of candidates who felt homosexuals were abominations or party insiders who spoke in reverential terms

of a Sunday morning televangelist. So successful was the media manipulation, in fact, that a wired-in guy like me was shocked, once in caucus, to see who had actually been elected.

But this much was clear by the afternoon of January 23—I was not cabinet material. In fact, I got the repeated sense that the Harperites could not care less if Halton was represented in the Conservative fold, if that meant Garth Turner became an MP. In fact, I later learned, they'd never expected to win the seat and would ensure it did not happen again, at least with me in it. Although I had yet to meet Doug Finley, I could feel his censure, and he obviously had a huge impact on Harper himself.

I could only wonder, then, what Harper wanted when he waved me up after the first caucus and told me to call his office for an audience. But then, I knew it wasn't going to be good.

In a few moments, ENG cameras filled the back of the caucus room, interspersed with still photographers, a few dozen reporters, and a handful of columnists and pundits. Burly members of the PM's RCMP detail positioned themselves between the media rabble and the members of caucus. Experienced journalists knew this was a ceremonial shot, a time-worn tradition allowing a rare glimpse inside the inner sanctum only when it was to the absolute advantage of those seated there. Few could have known that a new era of media manipulation was about to begin, or that the country was set to gain a leader so fundamentally committed to denying its citizens daily knowledge of the actions of its own government. But within five minutes the wars had begun.

Invited speakers included Ray Speaker, as well as Pierre Vincent and Charlie Mayer, Mulroney-era cabinet-level former MPs who were given time to brief the first Conservative caucus since two hundred

Progressive Conservative members sat in this room in the fall of 1993. I had always liked Charlie, one of the few genuine people in the halcyon days of Mulroney majority rule, who complemented his job as agricultural minister and man responsible for the wheat board with beat-up brown cowboy boots and western-style suits. I'd last seen him on one of my financial seminar speaking tours through Alberta five years earlier, when he showed up in the audience.

Today, after the cameras departed, Charlie was blunt, and his message dovetailed in with the theme that would dominate this caucus: don't talk to the media. The media is out to distort and misconstrue your words. The media will destroy you. The media will attack this government. The media has an agenda, and it is anti-government. Worse, it's anti-Conservative.

To me, it was alarmingly consistent with what I had just seen on the campaign trail. The Finley-orchestrated effort had been Janus-like in its dealings with the media, relying upon it to faithfully carry tightly scripted messages against carefully constructed backdrops and yet not trusting a single member of the pack of starved wolves who trailed the Harper wagons across the country. In many ways, the Finley-ordered TelePrompter was symbolic of the control, the discipline, and the defence against the inherent messiness and unpredictability of the democratic process.

Everywhere Harper went, the big box went with him. Inside were the two stand-up clear plastic panels that reflected the text of the speech being scrolled on the two black-and-white monitors below. Also in the box was the clear plastic podium that travelled to every event, along with the snap-in plastic side panels for the water glass. And while I had often seen Mulroney insist on his favourite podium— the green one with the Government of Canada coat of arms on the front—showing up with him, the TelePrompter was a new twist. Harper, an accomplished speaker and thinker and political practitioner, nonetheless was forced into a dependency on this thing that regimented his speeches and had the media accompanying him tuning out after the first words, already heard four times that day.

At a late-campaign event in Burlington, the crowd of five hundred was kept waiting twenty minutes while campaign workers scrambled to get the box to the front of the room, the podium rushed together, and the cabling in place before Harper was waved in. It was a particularly crucial rally, featuring a feeble but feisty Bill Davis, long-time former PC premier of Ontario, who was there to make Harper look less scary, less Reform, in a part of the GTA–905 belt where the party was hoping to make serious inroads, and where my door-knocking had told me fear of the neo-Cons abounded.

Part of the messaging that night involved the use of children, several of whom sat on the carpeted hotel riser at Harper's feet while he spoke. Directly in front of me, one of them insisted on banging her feet back and forth during the talk, until she succeeded in disconnecting the coaxial cable connecting the two monitors feeding the plastic display panels.

The TelePrompter went black, unknown to the techies who could not see it from their vantage point. Harper stuttered an imperceptible amount, and continued his stump speech—already delivered countless times—looking down now at the printed text placed in the three-ring binder before him on the podium. Laureen Harper was next to me. I could sense her growing panic, staring over her husband's shoulder into the darkness where the words should have been. She started looking around discreetly for help, but none was near. The evil child continued to swing her legs and thwack her feet, and now had attracted the attention of a photographer who lay prone on his belly getting a shot of her cuteness with a looming, irritated Harper behind.

But it was not going well. Rivulets of sweat had started to appear on the back of the leader's neck, darkening the top of his blue shirt collar. He miscued a joke about Davis, because it was new material and required looking down. Laureen grimaced a little through a smile.

The two of them were completely in sync, feeling the stress, aching over the words yet to come, trying to get through an event that should have been routine, unremarkable, forgettable, here in the rain-soaked Toronto hinterland at a time of night when road warriors like them are normally thinking about the room service menu.

Harper made the decision to dump a bunch of pages, cut his losses, and get out. The crowd was with him late in a campaign that gave every indication of going well. What would Doug Finley have told him, in that thick Scottish burr of his? Donna fuck it up, Stephen. They won' remember this tamorro.

And they didn't. The media took no notice, having tuned out when the speech started. Instead those few reporters who still had to file tonight were trying to find something new in this suburban crowd to report on. That ended up being Davis, former icon of moderation, who found himself in a scrum, while Laureen was handing her husband a tissue.

Back in caucus, Charlie Mayer was at the podium now, and it was clear thirteen years was too long to be out of it. Most people in the room had absolutely no idea who he was and, frankly, didn't care. Some old guy without power. But he soldiered on, delivering the one message this group would hear at least a dozen times in the two hours since the last camera guy had walked backwards through the doors into the Hall of Honour. Don't trust reporters. Don't talk to them.

"Whenever I see microphones in front of me," he finished with a final flourish, "I see daggers."

I walked into the prime minister's office.

It was 6:15 p.m. and snow whipped against the outside stone walls of Centre Block. Downstairs the reception was thinning and the food plates decimated. Upstairs, the door closed behind me, and Harper approached. We shook hands. There were a few small words about the campaign in my riding and we stood during them, while Hill watched. The prime minister then motioned me to sit down, which we did on either side of a small wooden end table with a brass lamp on it.

The PM's corner office on the third floor of the Centre Block is not the grandest on the Hill, but it radiates power. The floor is in hand-tooled herringbone-patterned hardwood and the walls are richly pan-elled. The soaring arched windows with their stone frames are covered with wooden shutters. In fact the entire room, when you look closely, is completely sealed off from external sight, to RCMP specifications. This office is more ceremonial than working, with the guts of the PMO operation taking place across the street in the bunker-like Langevin Block, the first federal government building erected off Parliament Hill. But this space serves well for receiving ambassadors, heads of state, and MPs about to be levitated into cabinet, or dashed upon the rocks of prime ministerial disdain.

My bottom was barely in the chair when Harper let it fly. I am very disappointed with you, he said. It got worse quickly, and the tone was unmistakable. Stephen Harper was condescending, belittling, and menacing. Here was a man with whom I had exchanged perhaps two hundred words in the last year, talking to a newly elected MP, a mem-ber of his own caucus, who had just succeeded in taking a riding from the Liberals after more than a decade—a riding that was a beachhead into the constituency-rich GTA—and he spoke to me as if I were a petulant, useless, idiot child.

His voice was without a single shred of respect. No acknowledg-ing I'd been in this office before, or in the cabinet room down the hall, or had run to be leader of a legacy party. It was as if Conservativism had started with the election of Stephen Harper as leader and led directly to this moment. Prior to that, he may have believed politicians bobbed like rudderless vessels on a sea of public opinion, blown helplessly by the winds of media know-it-alls. And he alone was out to change that.

And amid the barrage I couldn't help but remember the first time I'd met the man, half a year before at his one and only campaign stop in Halton. His handlers had wanted us to take him to a daycare, but we opted for a new housing construction site, because real estate was the one thing people in the region worshipped. It had been the engine of the local economy, and Conservative promises to cut the GST and usher in apprentice programs were wildly popular with buyers and builders.

The white minivan rolled up amid the half-built houses, screened with a giant picture of the leader's face and emblazoned with "Stand up for Canada" on the side. It was exciting, as the arrival of a leader always is. The door slid open, Harper emerged, and was about a foot taller than I had imagined. His people immediately whisked us all into the construction hut to avoid a scrum with the half-dozen reporters gathered in the dusty July heat, where we were fitted with leather tool belts and white hard hats.

"Is this a problem?" he asked.

His aides assured him it was not. The hat looked okay. He's sensitive, a woman whispered to me, after that awful cowboy shot in Calgary a few days ago. That photo would haunt him for months: a Calgarian, paunchy in a black leather vest, hands effeminately on his hips, wearing his Stetson backwards.

We did the event, which involved walking around being photographed, and then we all piled into the van to head for lunch at a neighbouring golf course. Harper rode shotgun and I was behind him. "So you were in Kim's cabinet?" he said without looking at me. And before I could answer he turned and asked, "How bad was it?"

What do you mean? I asked.

"How bad was it, losing it all, getting killed like that?" he said. He was smiling now, and it struck me that his one and only vision of the candidate in the van with him was of a former Progressive Conservative who, by a fluke, had managed to survive the ethnic cleansing of 1993. A curiosity of conflict, like the wrinkled Japanese infantryman who emerges from a cave on a Pacific atoll forty-nine years after the war ended, wondering who won.

"That must have been quite the surprise, I would guess," and he looked off at the stream of subdivision houses now flying by in the thirty-degree heat outside. I said nothing. There was no point. But Stephen Harper had succeeded in an instant in making me feel old and irrelevant. More telling, in this, our first encounter: he had just divided the inside of that white van into PC and Reform. It was deft.

The prime minister was at me now about my comments on Emerson, and I explained my opposition to floor-crossing MPs and my position that despite the new minister's worth and experience, the ethical action would be to re-submit to the people. How, I asked, could you have been critical of what Belinda did, and now turn around and cause this to happen?

Harper glared. He pointed out to me that he had not voted for legislation in the last Parliament that would have banned floor-crossing (although half his caucus did). He said there had been nothing in the election campaign platform that prevented an MP from abandoning a party, or the voters, to pursue his or her own agenda. That, he said, leaning forward and staring hard at me, was not his position, and I was absolutely wrong in talking to anyone about it. Pointedly, he did not mention Belinda's name. I thought the better part of valour at the moment was to follow suit. But it also struck me:

here was a man hiding behind semantics, convinced his position was unassailable because words defended him. He may have hinted broadly that Belinda was a weak person of questionable intellect that led her to make the wrong decision in leaving his side. But he never actually said the process was incorrect. In an argument of logic, he won. So when I said, "I still find this position unprincipled," he needed only to look at me with disdain.

He was done with that. We moved on to me. It was not going well.

Harper said he felt he could not trust me. "To put it charitably, you were independent during the campaign." The penny was dropping now. The dots between anonymous on-the-phone Doug Finley, worries about my blog, and the leader's ear were filling in rapidly. He turned to look squarely at me and said, "I don't need a media star in my caucus."

Media star. The choice of words was interesting. I had come to my candidacy as a businessman, employer, and entrepreneur, running three companies. I thought the man would have known that, realized I had not been an on-camera personality for a few years, or a daily newspaper columnist for decades. But perhaps some sins could never be expunged.

The prime minister paused. "I was going to offer you something, a role, something I had that is delicate, something important," he said. "But now I'm not going to anymore. Instead we will just see what happens, what you do, over the next few weeks."

The prime minister looked over at me, waiting for my face to react. Was he seeking disappointment, anger, or regret? Remorse, maybe? A desperate cry for forgiveness? Stephen Harper had just dangled some valued, unnamed position or title, then snatched it away.

(Only three years later, when I heard on CTV that Stephen Harper cheered at news of my defeat in the 2008 election, would I realize what a pivotal moment was passing.)

But I was not here to ask for anything. He had nothing I wanted.

The only goal pursued had been to become a member of Parliament, and my behaviour, principles, or beliefs could not be changed with a job offer.

I started to rise out of my chair. "Well," I said, "I guess that's it then..."

But Harper wasn't done yet. "Sit down.

"You're a journalist," he said, "and we all know journalists make bad politicians. Politicians know how to stick to a message. That's how they are successful. Journalists think they always have to tell the truth."

Dorothy's face was etched with worry as I emerged. "Let's go," I said, taking her hand. We went past the guards, down the stone staircase, pulled on our winter coats, and stepped into the wind sweeping cruelly around the corner of Centre Block.

Harper's motorcade was there, lights on in all five vehicles, clouds of exhaust swirling around the back of the Cadillac, the two suvs, and the chase cars. Obviously those MPS' wives still waiting in the reception room to meet the prime minister would be kept waiting until they gave up.

We got back to the condo and, utterly drained by the confrontational nature of the evening, Dorothy checked out and went to bed. The BlackBerry was now buzzing constantly, as urgent media requests and emails of support soon overflowed the mailbox. Esther was still at the constituency office where people kept showing up, wanting to hang out. She was obviously upset, but bravely encouraging. "We're all with you," she said on the phone, "and so proud of you." Unsaid was "But why are you doing this?" She couldn't be expected to understand, knowing nothing of the talk with Harper. Then George Paisiovich called; he was my long-time and irreverent political mentor, former EA, and afterwards my chief of staff as revenue minister. He laughed. "You're fucked," he giggled. "What took you so long?"

It was the night of February 9, three days after the Harper government was sworn in, the day of the first formal caucus meeting, and day one of the triumphant return of Conservatives to Ottawa after wandering, shattered, in the political wilderness. It was also the renaissance of my political career, my return to public life—this time on a crusade for a chance to take the ethical and principled position, epitomized by a blunt and unvarnished online dialogue. And George was right, I was already screwed.

Outside, the snow blew fiercely across George Street, swirling around the people tripping from bar to bar in the Byward market. Of course, I sat and tried to gain some perspective. I got elected after a huge effort. Went to Ottawa, sideswiped like everyone by Emerson and Fortier. Got scrummed, had a choice, wrote a blog, told the truth. Now, I was probably finished.

And how could it have been avoided? Use the members' entrance instead of the centre doors to duck the media pack? Wave the reporters off, say "No comment" and pick up speed down the stone corridor, the way I saw newly minted ministers Carol Skelton and Diane Finley do? Support the leader by praising Emerson and, in so doing, negate my one reason for coming here? Turn down Mike Duffy's request to do that five o'clock hit in the foyer?

Or perhaps it was more profound. Maybe it was a mistake attempting to become an MP again; I was too old and unencumbered by ambition to lie anymore. Too jaded to believe that any philosophy, any party, any team, any leader had all the answers. Maybe there'd been too much hypocrisy and artifice on the campaign trail—too many crass Doug Finley manipulations—to believe these guys were about anything other than the seizing of power. Maybe it was my embrace of the new technology, the communications channel that now, I could see, would open up the entire political process and be the greatest threat to leaders.

Bundled figures formed a short line to get into The Black Tomato, and I assumed at least a few of them were Conservatives out on a tear. They had a lot to celebrate, having been handed the reins. Newly minted Tory ministers would now ride in black hybrids with drivers, while Liberals with household names were forced to share the little green buses plying Parliament Hill along with the couriers, cleaners, and translators. Caucus members would tell constituents they were in the room with The Big Guy, enjoying unequalled access to those who ran the country, and conferred with them in doing so. But in the end, as my chat with Harper underscored, it was all about power. Getting it, using it, and keeping it. I sensed a widespread national disappointment was in its naissance.

Emerson was a wake-up call. Stephen Harper, marketed as the principled "unpolitician," the academic and theory-driven citizen, who had once turned his back on public life in disgust to pursue an agenda of commonsense policy initiatives, had turned out to be a surprise. Did he really believe that telling the truth and being a politician were mutually exclusive? Was he so sure he could change my mind by offering a position in his government? Was he being dishonest in allowing Belinda Stronach to be portrayed as weak and deficient for changing parties, or was he being dishonest now in embracing a political weathervane like David Emerson?

George told me to quit, trigger a by-election, and run as an independent. It was a bizarre conversation, in many respects, two weeks and two days after standing in front of the cameras in Milton, with the New Hollywood rock band playing wildly behind me. Ever the seer, George was convinced Harper would end up a failure. He was even more convinced I was in for a shit-kicking.

At midnight I wrote a blog entry that the next day would be

picked up by the mainstream media and seal my fate. It was printed in its entirety by the *National Post* and *Ottawa Citizen*, and included in the morning press clipping binder at the PMO.

First, I'd like to thank all the people who took a moment to drop me a line over the past few hours, and those who have come by and left a comment here. Mostly I'd like to thank the five volunteers who showed up tonight in Milton to help Sharon and Esther unpack all the stuff that arrived from the outgoing Halton MP's office. Boy, having more than one secondhand computer and a geriatric printer is going to be sweet.

Speaking of offices, after today I'm expecting the whip will be assigning me a renovated washroom somewhere in a forgotten corner of a vermin-infested dank basement in Ottawa. That should go well with my seat in the House of Commons that will be visible only during lunar eclipses.

Uh-huh. That kind of a day. This one MP came face-to-face with the party machine in a series of unhappy meetings including one tonight with the prime minister. I think it is now safe to say my career options within the Conservative caucus are seriously limited. If you would like a course on how not to be popular in Ottawa, then take a seat.

I have written here many times over the past few months about my journey to become an MP again, and why I wanted to return to Ottawa. It was not to be a minister with a limo, but, as I explained, to try and empower elected people more, to make them relevant and free, so the voters would also become more empowered. And I campaigned to advance issues my middle class voters are so concerned with—things those families need and want.

But, I arrived as the prime minister was appointing a floor-crossing Liberal and an unelected party official to his cabinet, which seemed to fly in the face of everything I had told voters about accountability and democracy. It also made me question the whole process, after eight months of knocking on doors to win my coveted seat in this magnificent stone building on the banks of the Ottawa River.

Going from door to door turns a politician into a democrat. At least, it did for me. By the time I got to Parliament Hill, I was infused with the spirit of a new era in government, sated on the belief we would see freedom reign in the Chamber and that the days of subjugation of MPs by the prime minister's office were numbered. I had swallowed with gusto promises of more free votes, more powerful committees of free-thinking MPs, more listening to the voters, and an elected and responsible Senate.

And, most importantly, I had taken that to the people. Change. The election was about change. I asked people in Halton to embrace the Conservatives as a modern, inclusive, mainstream, principled party of honest people committed to changing the system for the better. Finally. Something worth knocking on doors for in the dark and the cold. Something to believe in. Something to run for. Something on the Hill worth coming back for with a passion.

Sure, I thought the appointment of those two ministers was questionable. And after stating many a time that Belinda Stronach should have sought a by-election after her defection, how could I not say the same obvious thing now? It was simple for my constitutents to understand, and simple for me. I did not seek the microphones out, but when they were under my nose and a clear question was asked, I gave a clear answer.

Everybody who makes up the government should be elected. They should be elected as members of the party that forms the government. Anybody who switches parties should go back to the people. To do otherwise is to place politicians above the people when, actually, it's the other way around.

But my comments were deemed not helpful, even though I chose them carefully and pulled some punches, suggesting Minister Emerson be given a little time before deciding on whether or not to get elected as a Tory.

Did I know the potential consequences of speaking my mind, or sticking with the principles that brought me to this cold hill? Yeah, I did. I have been an MP before, and a leadership candidate and a cabinet minister. I have the hide to prove it. I know the PMO has a song sheet it wants all caucus members to sing from, and I know what happens when an individual chooses to go his or her own way. I was just hoping this time I would not be asked to choose—between party and principle.

I chose principle. My deepest loyalty is to what I believe, what I told the voters, and what I want Parliament to become. The Emerson affair may indeed blow over. The minister may decide not to take the heat. David may turn into a cabinet star and a national asset. But he should still have the conviction to get elected a member of the team he chose. The same team that I chose, and fought like a warrior to join, helped by hundreds more and supported by tens of thousands of others. How could any member of caucus not privately feel the same?

A few nights ago, I made some pledges here. I pledged to remember that my job is not to serve the party or the prime minister, but rather the people who sent me here. I pledged to work to enhance the position of MP, because when that happens, the voters win. I pledged to share my MP's power with you every way I could, and to speak up for middle-class Canadians.

That voice may be a little fainter now, coming from that forgotten basement washroom office, but, dammit, it won't quit.

✦

By mid-morning the sheet of paper on the kitchen counter was covered with the names and phone numbers of media people requesting interviews. Canadian Press had reprinted most of last night's blog entry and sent it out on the wire. It was the beginning of months in which postings would end up in editorials and news stories, substitutes for actual interviews. It was further proof the blog had become a major tool of communications, with the power to save my political ass or destroy me.

The phone rang. "This is the prime minister's office," a woman announced. "I have the prime minister's chief of staff on the line. Please hold."

Ian Brodie had been at both of the caucus meetings since the election. At thirty-eight, he was slight, somewhat rumpled, with lightly combed blond hair and a sparse beard. He carried a notebook with him, spoke little, and was far less imposing a figure than the older, larger, and louder Doug Finley. Together, they were Stephen Harper's deep back room—his advisors, practitioners, and enforcers. Brodie would last until the summer of 2008.

Brodie and Harper had met as students sixteen years earlier, at the University of Calgary. Brodie was a political science grad studying under the libertarian Ted Morton, who would later become a Ralph Klein cabinet minister and take a serious—and, to many moderates, alarming—run at the premiership in 2006. Harper was studying economics, already organizing for the Reform Party, and would soon graduate to go into the oil and gas business, working for his father.

Brodie moved on to eventually score a junior professorship in 1997 at Western in London, Ontario, where he drifted into Reform Party politics the next year. He helped organize for Preston Manning, and then became president of the Canadian Alliance riding association in London West, where he was the assistant campaign manager for failed candidate Salim Mansur. That year he also married Vida, an events planner at the university.

Two years later Brodie managed to become a tenured professor, but a year later quit to go to Harper. He became assistant chief of staff for the newly elected Alliance leader, after having worked on his leadership campaign in charge of tours. After Harper's subsequent election as leader of the new Conservative Party in 2004, Brodie and Finley were instrumental in crafting the new organization, Brodie as executive director and Finley as director of political operations. In May 2005, following the defection of Belinda Stronach and Harper's failed attempt to bring down the Martin Liberals, Finley seized control of the national campaign organization, vowing not to repeat the mistakes of the disastrous 2004 election campaign. Brodie took over the operation of the Office of the Leader of the Opposition, which he described at the time as "a fucking disaster."

"This is Ian Brodie. I have Jay Hill, the government whip, here with me."

It was mid-morning, and I had promised many media outlets I'd tell them shortly whether or not interviews would happen. After the events of the previous evening nothing was exactly clear. Pathetically, I imagined the Brodie call that was about to take place would extend an olive branch. Dorothy sat a few feet away, and she started to look hopeful.

"I'm a blunt person," Brodie said. "I heard your comments on *Canada* AM, and this freelance commenting of yours has to end. The public undermining has to end. There was nothing in our platform that was against floor-crossing. If you want to fuck with us, we will certainly fuck with you. Do you want to sit as an independent? Then we can arrange that. Count on it."

The tone was shocking, the words driven by an obvious anger. Whatever was going on in the PMO that morning, it was emotional and unequivocal, taken seriously enough to draw in the top players. Harper's assessment of our evening meeting had clearly been negative.

I tried a compromise, and offered to turn down any further media interviews. Jay Hill spoke. "That is unacceptable," he said. "You are damaging your colleagues and the prime minister. You will do no more media." Then he asked me, simply, why I was saying the appointment of David Emerson was wrong.

"Because that's what I believe," I said. Hill laughed.

"Let me make this clear." Brodie's voice dropped a bit and he slowed. "I am telling you, you will not give any more media interviews. I am telling you, you will stop writing the blog. And I'm telling you that you'll issue a press release today praising the prime minister's appointment of Emerson. Are you clear?"

Yes, I said. Clear.

It was clear that a political staffer, unelected and unaccountable, answering directly to the prime minister, had just tried to gag a member of Parliament, threatened to throw him out of the party he'd been elected by the people to represent and ordered him to make a false statement.

Oh my God. Here we go.

CHAPTER THREE

"I was there when it happened."

—Peter Near, blogger, Halton, Ontario

THE BACK OF WALLY BUTTS'S VAN, seriously in need of a wash, was filled with clear plastic bags full of Stephen Harper buttons and window stickers saying "Stand up for Canada." A few of them spilled out as the car door slid open and that gap-toothed smile of his was briefly visible.

Butts might make the perfect political operative, if only for his deep improbability. From the top of his thin grey brush cut down to his workers' boots, he seems the antithesis of a well-oiled political machine. Wally is not young, not slender, not well-spoken, and decidedly uncharismatic. He looks, perpetually, as if he just climbed down from a combine, even when cleaned up and in a suit jacket. And he has the kind of eyes that seem incapable of artifice. He lives in a small village in Norfolk County, and is religious about returning each night to his own rural bed, even when that means driving four hours from a distant event in the godless GTA.

In the summer of 2006, the Conservative Party of Canada increased Butts's territory in vote-rich southern Ontario to include the swath of ridings from Welland through to the Etobicoke Creek, an improbable mishmash of deep rural and intense urban constituencies with a smattering of Tory MPS and a mess of city people the party seemed to be losing patience with. His job was a complicated one, and involved ensuring riding associations were raising desperately needed cash;

that acceptable candidates were recruited; that a landscape of changing party rules and directives were adhered to; that Stephen Harper was a constant and growing presence in every community newspaper in every town; that party memberships were being flogged at all opportunities and rosters maintained; that revenue-generating party polling packages were being sold to the locals; that the party-run data base, called CIMS, was not only subscribed to but fed with every morsel of information so that, at any moment, Ottawa could have eyes on the locals; and, above all, that Doug Finley was happy. Or at least not pissed. Close enough.

Wally clambered out of the van. It was ten in the morning on an early summer's day—a Thursday—seven months before the federal election of January 2006. Stephen Harper was embarking on his "Summer of Love" barbecue tour amid widespread media snickers, just a few weeks after failing to defeat the Martinites (thanks to that damn Belinda) and Wally was tasked with this particular stage of the "secondary tour." This morning it led to a parking lot behind the bar on Main Street in downtown Milton, Ontario. The lot was empty, as was Main Street and, in fact, Milton. Esther had worked for four days to try to come up with something, anything, for the tour to do.

"Why a Thursday morning?" she belted into the phone. "Why are we wasting all this time on trotting around two politicians nobody has ever heard of, in a place that's deserted? What genius up there thought this one up?" In the end, it would be a pathetic walkabout for Conservative MP Gord Brown and party stalwart John Reynolds to a decorating store, then a lawyer's office, and finally a barbershop where Mike, the gregarious clipper—and our best shot at a photo op—had forgotten about the tour and taken the morning off. We mainstreeted a bit, the two TV camera guys trailing looking bored out of their skulls, and ran into three ancient women who enthusiastically said Mr. Harper scared them. Wally was appalled. We all retreated to the van and fled one exit down the 401 to the bucolic hamlet of Campbellville, where the only people we could find were in a store, and lived in Toronto. Damn.

Wally's forte is The Pitch. He lives to give it—getting up after a potluck banquet at the Legion or in the arena—gripping the handheld microphone like a Vegas crooner, flashing that tooth-challenged smile, flipping the cord in the other, pacing and pitching. His surprisingly easy showmanship in front of a crowd and seamless patter are disarming and unexpected. As a result, he manages to part people and their money in a legendary fashion, spelling out the tax advantages of supporting a political party—especially one that avowedly hates taxes.

Wally Butts is a Conservative Party of Canada (CPC) regional organizer, one of a small but quite professional army maintained by Finley across the country. He's paid, party people say, well into the six figures to cajole, organize, promote, observe, and report. On the day his dirty van delivered Reynolds and Brown to us, Wally commanded a serious amount of respect—a situation that would, in the tumultuous months ahead, be blown violently apart.

(One night a year later at Troy's Diner, also in Milton, with the party deeply involved in a secret operation to unhorse the sitting Conservative MP, Wally would incite a near-riot among the local party members. He'd champion a Doug Finley directive mandating a search committee be struck to find candidates, even though it was just six months after the election that had replaced a Liberal in Halton with a Tory for the first time in thirteen years. With a straight face and all the rural credibility he could muster, he told them the decision to have every party MP challenged for his or her own job had been "approved by caucus." Whether Wally knew it was an outright lie or had been told by Finley it was a fact was moot. Everyone in the room knew no caucus member, newly elected or otherwise, would approve a plan to trigger a nomination race for their own seat. It was a minority Parliament. It was bizarre.

("Screw you," president Pat Whyte said, as he ended the meeting angrily. Months later, Whyte would be forced to choose between me and the party. He chose the party.)

In the dusty parking lot behind the bar, Wally stooped, picked up the bag of Harper buttons, and handed them to me, as John Reynolds and Gord Brown climbed out of his crowded back seat. The secondary tour was about to begin. Reynolds, the legendary Reform Party operative, former smooth-talking BC radio show host, long-time MP, and nobody in the GTA, was leaving politics to sit as the honorary chair of the election campaign to come. He was predictably charming, aloof, and effective. Gord Brown seemed to be a tour afterthought; he was the MP for Leeds-Grenville, a local hotelier virtually unknown outside of his hometown of Gananoque, Ontario—just down the 401 from Brockville, a place made famous to social historians as the city where early Reformers danced on a Quebec flag while Brian Mulroney was trying to effect the Meech Lake Accord.

It wasn't clear, actually, why this tour was taking place, or why the politically inconsequential Gord Brown was standing in the back lot of the Ivy Arms shaking my hand. That did not become clear until many months later, after I'd walked into the elevator on the sixth floor of the Justice Building, just off Parliament Hill, and sought out his office, two floors above mine. By that time, the spring of 2006, Stephen Harper had hand-picked Brown to be the chair of his largest and most powerful regional caucus, Ontario. It was shortly after the train wreck of a caucus meeting, the first one, that Brown called me up to his office for a little chat.

Gord Brown is a man who does not quickly stand out in a crowd, which may have helped make him a successful small-town politician, the kind Stephen Harper does well with. He served two terms on Gananoque (pop. 4,900) town council, was chairman of the St. Lawrence Parks Commission, twice headed the local chamber of commerce, and raised money to build a beach in town. In 2000 he abandoned roots as a Progressive Conservative and ran as a Canadian

Alliance candidate, narrowly losing to Liberal Joe Jordan. Four years later, as a Harper Conservative, he took Leeds-Grenville, and was quickly made vice-chair of the Ontario caucus. In that election campaign he was touted by Hugh Segal as "a minister from eastern Ontario in the next Conservative government."

"You should be less ambitious," Brown told me, sitting in his office before a giant map of the electoral results. "You should try harder to get along. A lot of these guys are suspicious of you, you know, with the media contacts you've got and the profile. Maybe you should spend some more time, and take a few of them out for dinner. Lie low, you know? Just stay out of the headlines, below the radar. Lay off the blog, and I'm sure over time things will change."

He added, unexpectedly, "They have to."

In the spring of that year I was in trouble, but there was still hope. By the summer, trouble had turned into shock and confusion for local Conservatives in my riding, as details of the suspected nomination pact between televangelist Charles McVety and Doug Finley emerged. By September, with my apparent defeat of the challenge from the righteous Right, the true scope of the Finley plan to dump me had surfaced. At that point, I was only a month away from the second attempt on my political life, the one that would succeed.

In Ottawa, Brown convened Ontario caucus at 8 a.m. on Wednesdays in the main meeting room, an hour and a half before the national meeting began in the same spot. Members were always late getting there, with maybe a dozen of the forty MPs huddled around the coffee table as the agenda started. Within a half hour, the numbers would triple, which meant items of any consequence were pushed back to get the best crowd.

In caucus, for some reason, people always sit in the same spots. In national, all Quebec MPs congregate in the third of the seats to the left of the podium, for example. Most non-francophone women MPs sit in a single row with each other on the right. Jim Flaherty picks a seat near the end of the second-last row by the coffee table. Peter MacKay mirrors that on the far side. Nova Scotian MPs gravitate to the single row of green chairs lining the back wall. Mike Chong sits on one of the two small benches near the fireplace with the iron gargoyles.

On the morning of September 20, Peter van Loan was in his usual Ontario caucus seat, in the front row, reading his usual *Time* magazine. Flaherty took off his suit jacket, as always, got a coffee, and sat in the second-last row. Harold Albrecht and Pat Davidson, along with David Tilson, were behind me in the centre section. On the right, near the back, were Gary Goodyear, Jeff Watson, Diane Finley, Guy Lauzon, Joe Preston, Gary Schellenberger and, to the right, uncharacteristically, Senator Marjory LeBreton. Slipping in to sit at the back near the main doors, just before nine o'clock, was Doug Finley.

Gord Brown stood at the prime minister's podium and called on Chuck Strahl. The gregarious minister and former Alliance rebel, imperceptibly fighting a form of lung cancer, struggled through a defence of the government agricultural policy before giving up. "The prime minister has pretty well made it clear," he said, "that we could be spending billions and the farmers would still be bitching. Maybe we ought to be just telling them how much better things are with us than under the Liberals for a change, instead of coming here to complain about it all." He was frustrated, as guys like Preston and Schellenberger and Larry Miller chewed away at his ankles and listed all the reasons producers would never vote for them again. Unlike at national caucus, MPs were allowed to take to the microphone at their regional gathering.

It was the first caucus meeting of the fall session, which had started in the wake of the shootings at Montreal's Dawson College. Two days earlier, I'd written and published this blog comment, immediately after Conservative MPs had endured a profoundly useless national caucus. It was impossible to know then how my words would later be used.

As it should have been, there was but one major story over the last couple of days in Ottawa, which was the fallout from the Dawson College shooting. PMSH talked about that at length in caucus, and it's all the reporters wanted to focus on, as well. I was scrummed about it a few times coming out of the national caucus room, and was struck that the questions were a lot less probing and confrontational than I'd have expected.

Maybe my political radar is clogged with sand right now, but I'd say the thing the freak (the shooter) did was enough to knock the Tory gun plan into a slough in Saskatchewan. After all, anti-gun sentiment runs no higher anywhere than in urban Montreal, for obvious reasons. The Conservatives have been counting on Quebec seats to counter the desert called Toronto.

The shooting at Dawson by a guy carrying three legal weapons shows the existing law is a crock. And the fact that this Goth with a death wish and a troubled background got firearm acquisition permits demonstrates our system is devoid of any common sense.

So, we have a multiple organ failure at the federal level. It makes me sick to think about the $1 billion in tax money spent to set up a system which gladly handed over a semi-auto killing machine to a mentally imbalanced psycho. Yeah, we can crap all over the Libs for doing that, but Tories are the government now. We have to fix it. And we won't get near the problem if some of my hats-and-horses colleagues continue to lament over farmers and duck hunters who want to blow holes in birds and animals for the simple joy of it.

After Strahl finished, Brown began what he called a "round table" and opened up the meeting's remaining twenty minutes to any topic. Jeff Watson, a former Chrysler worker and now MP for a Windsor-area riding, got up and went to the floor mic on the right. I paid him scant attention, but it was quite unusual to see him on his feet. Besides, the last time we'd interacted, it had not been constructive.

Back then, at the summer caucus retreat in Cornwall, I sat behind Watson for a while, noticing the huge amount of nervous energy the young MP showed. His right foot was in a constant state of tapping, which made most of his body move. Watson was the only guy in torn blue jeans that day, which, along with his sideburns, were maybe meant to reinforce his youthful thirty-five years, or the fact he was the first guy elected to Parliament who worked the trim line at Daimler's Windsor car plant. Actually, he was the first autoworker ever to sit in the Commons.

Like Brown, he'd first been elected in 2004, after running as a Reform candidate twice against Herb Gray in Windsor West, where he was crushed with 14 percent of the vote in 1997 and 23 percent in 2000. Then in 2004 he switched ridings and managed to squeak by Susan Whelan in Essex by less than a thousand votes; he widened that to three thousand when she tried to regain the seat in January 2006.

In Cornwall I'd pitched the group on pension-splitting, promoting the early October conference I'd organized for the West Block, making the case for allowing retired couples to share pension revenue for tax purposes. Brown was supportive, as were Helena Guergis, Pierre Poilievre, Colin Carrie, and others. Rick Norlock spoke against it, saying it wasn't government policy, so it should not be supported. Also in opposition to the policy that Jim Flaherty would announce nine weeks later were Diane Finley, Doug's wife and then minister of human resources, along with Peterborough's Dean Del Mastro, Dean Allison, Royal Galipeau, and, surprisingly, Flaherty himself.

Then Watson spoke, and silenced the room with his anger. "My generation is just sick and tired of paying the bills for you baby boomers," he said to me from the opposite end of the table. "It's the 'me' generation—you guys—who have saddled us with all this debt, and the last thing we should be doing is giving you greedy bastards any more money."

Brown, sitting beside me, looked worried. I made a poor joke to cut the tension. "Man, you must have been pretty pissed at your parents . . ." The room laughed.

Moments later, the session over, Watson was at my elbow saying loudly that I had no right to speak to him that way. "You know nothing of my parents," he said. Of course not, I replied, it was a throwaway line. Sorry, pal.

He was at the mic now, a month later, and his words once again shut the room down. "I'm putting forward a motion to have Garth Turner removed from caucus," he said.

Should the next twenty minutes have been expected? In hindsight, probably. Over the summer of 2006 I'd used the "hats-and-horses" shorthand on my blog for the western, rural, Reform, social conservatives who dominate Harper's caucus. That phrase, by the way, had been coined by Hugh Segal, former chief of staff to Brian Mulroney, former leadership contender of the Progressive Conservative Party, and now a senator and rumoured chief Harper on-the-bus advisor during the campaign. Immediately after the January election he called me and made a point of clarifying that "contrary to what you might have read in the media, I have absolutely no influence now with the hats-and-horses crowd."

Firearms control and the dismantling of the long gun registry was but one emerging issue in that late summer. Another was the government's looming first green plan, and the apparent dominance of those who worried about the energy-sucking economic engine of the oil sands far more than climate change. Then there was same-sex marriage, McVety and the religious Right, and the constant tension that was engendering.

At an Ontario caucus meeting on August 29 in Owen Sound—Larry Miller's riding—my presentation on the nomination battle in my riding, which drew a line between party headquarters and the McVety forces that tried to defeat me, found absolutely no sympathy.

"I think that was your own fault," MP Cheryl Gallant said. "You stirred up the pot. You stuck a stick in McVety's eye." Two years earlier, Cheryl had impacted the 2004 Conservative election campaign by comparing abortion in Canada to beheadings in Iraq. To my surprise, in that caucus meeting she was supported by John Baird, treasury board president and a known supporter of same-sex marriage, which McVety—as president of Defend Marriage Canada—was out to destroy.

Gord Brown took me aside in Owen Sound and, paternally, said there was "a huge amount of animosity" against me at that moment, which was the direct result of a statement made during my nomination battle fourteen days before. "That is why they're after you," he said, "and it is very, very serious. I don't know if I can stop it, and if I were you, I'd certainly apologize, and I would do it today."

I recalled that on August 25, in the very middle of the Halton nomination fight, Canadian Press ran this story, which said, in part:

OTTAWA (CP)—The unholy war of words over gay marriage between outspoken Conservative MP Garth Turner and some members of Canada's Christian community has evolved into a full-fledged fight for who gets to represent his riding in the next election.

Turner's opponents were to hold a meeting Tuesday night to determine if they could run someone against him in the upcoming nomination meeting in the riding of Halton. The Conservative party does not protect incumbent MPs.

Turner accuses anti-same-sex marriage advocates in particular of taking advantage of the slow summer months to try and stack the nomination meeting scheduled for September 11.

In the meantime, he says he's "full of vinegar."

"Am I supposed to change my mind and all of a sudden hate homosexual people because I'm facing a challenge in my riding? Of course not, I'm not going to change." Turner said in an interview.

"I'm still the member of Parliament, and I'm going to do what I said I'm going to do. They're not going to threaten me, they're not going to scare me, and my tail is not between my legs."

A few minutes later, in the meeting room at the Best Western Owen Sound, the Ontario caucus heard an apology. "The published comment was not in any way meant to suggest that people who oppose same-sex marriage are anti-homosexual. It was not directed at anyone in this room."

But the damage was done.

Jeff Watson's motion just hung there for a moment. He didn't explain it, rationalize it, support it. He just said it. "I'm putting forward a motion to have Garth Turner removed from caucus."

Brown was off his game. "What?" he said. "Why are you doing this?" Watson took the mic again and accused me of using my blog to break caucus confidentiality. He gave no specifics, but said, "My privileges as a member are being compromised. I'm afraid to speak now because I just don't know if everything I say is being written and will be published that night." It was hard just at the moment to think of anything Watson had ever said in caucus worth blogging about, save at the Cornwall meeting.

Brown was still trying to recover, instantly aware of the implication of the motion and the significance of it happening inside his meeting.

Kicking a caucus member out was hugely serious, unheard of just a few months after an election, and passing strange in a minority government environment. "I . . . I had no notice of this motion," he said, "and I'm not sure we should be discussing it like this." He truly seemed surprised, out of the loop.

Several members were at the mic now, ready to pile on and support Watson—Gary Goodyear of Cambridge and Scott Reid from Eastern Ontario first among them. Reid, as it turned out, would turn into a key promoter of the caucus suspension, and is one of the few MPs on either side of the House I have never actually spoken to.

Reid was a Preston Manning advisor in the 1990s then worked as a researcher for the Reform Party for three years, afterward joining Alliance leader Stockwell Day as a speechwriter and organizer. In 2002 he defected to Stephen Harper, becoming his chief Ontario organizer in the campaign that saw Harper defeat Day; he then ran the Harper transition team. Harper appointed him to be lead negotiator in merger talks with Peter MacKay's PCs, and encouraged him to run in the 2004 campaign, at which time he provoked a national furor by repeating his previously published view that official bilingualism should be scrapped. Reid's family business is Giant Tiger Stores Ltd., where he also worked. During the 2006 campaign, Stephen Harper used a company store as the backdrop for a major policy announcement.

Reid and three other members spoke in support of Watson, two against. Two more asked why this motion was "coming out of nowhere." Brown, flustered, ruled it out of order, but identified it as "grave." He announced that a special meeting would be convened to discuss it. In the House, during Question Period that day, he told me that the event would be taking place in one hour in the cabinet committee room. I called my office and asked that the last hundred blog entries be printed, punched, put into a binder, and rushed over.

The very words, I thought, will defend me. As it turned out, that binder—furiously assembled—would never be opened.

By 4 p.m. the cabinet committee room—I had not been in here since Jay Hill chewed me out in early February—was filling smartly. In total, twenty-eight MPs showed up, and about half of them spoke. The meeting lasted less than an hour. The initial conversation dealt with the allegation that my words had breached caucus confidentiality, which was serious. If it were true that I had published conversations or comments that compromised the secrecy of the caucus room, then I deserved to be expelled. I agreed.

Of course, leaking caucus proceedings is a time-honoured fact of life on the Hill. Not a week goes by that statements made in any of the major caucuses do not end up in the notebooks of parliamentary reporters. In many instances, the PMO itself is the source.

For example, during the height of the spring 2006 flag flap, when Harper was being sharply criticized for not allowing the Peace Tower flag to be half-masted when combat deaths took place in Afghanistan, it was reported that caucus gave him a standing ovation the day he clarified his position. Canadian Press moved the story and it ended up in virtually every daily. It was a crock.

There was no ovation, standing or otherwise. In case I had dozed off, I queried three other caucus members, all of whom confirmed my observation: nobody clapped. The PMO made it up. The PMO leaked it.

The next day, CP's Ottawa bureau chief confirmed that information of this kind is never verified, never confirmed, because of the inherent difficulty in doing so.

When young Michael Chong quit his job as intergovernmental affairs minister because he fundamentally disagreed, as did I, with the Harper motion to recognize the Quebecois as a nation, within days he would be savaged in the media. Harper "insiders" told the *Toronto Star* exactly how he quit, what he did before he quit, when he quit, and how the prime minister felt about it.

Divulging information only cabinet-level officials would have, they painted the principled Chong as a selfish renegade who deceived Harper and thereby seriously betrayed his colleagues. It was a deliberate leak, done for deliberate purposes. And it was effective.

Days later, in a very exhaustive leak to *The Hill Times*, the PMO described through a caucus member, Tom Lukiwski, the gushing reaction Stephen Harper received on Wednesday morning, November 22, 2006, when he first told MPs and ministers about his plan for the Quebecois motion. Lukiwski not only revealed the contents of the prime minister's remarks, but described in some detail his colleagues' alleged response, which included at least two of them weeping openly.

Tory MP Tom Lukiwski told *The Hill Times*:

"I do know this. When he discussed his motion in caucus, our Quebec members of Parliament were absolutely overjoyed. I mean there was a couple of them frankly who had tears in their eyes," Mr. Lukiwski (Regina-Lumsden-Lake Centre, Sask.) said last week following Question Period on the Hill. When asked whether he was overstating the facts, Mr. Lukiwski said: "I'm not kidding."

Lukiwski, first elected in 2004 by 122 votes, became parliamentary secretary to the leader of the government in the House of Commons and minister for democratic reform. In the spring of 1998 he made national headlines when a twenty-year-old tape emerged showing him, as a young political organizer, making graphic homophobic remarks. His abject Commons apology was immediately accepted by Stephen Harper.

But this afternoon, in this room just off Harper's office, hinting at what happened in caucus was a capital offence. As the speakers' list lengthened, I asked the group for specific examples of what confidences my blog entries might have betrayed. I shoved the thick white binder with its chronologically arranged and tabbed postings across the table.

"Show me."

Nobody reached for the book. "Your comments are thinly veiled references to what may have happened in caucus," Goodyear said. "You know, that the prime minister may have spoken on an issue, or that an issue was on the agenda—that crosses the line."

And that was pretty much it. My specific crime appeared to come down to this sentence: "There was but one major story over the last couple of days in Ottawa, which was the fallout from the Dawson College shooting. Harper talked about that at length in caucus." But it quickly became apparent that the real issue was not confidentiality at all. "We play as a team or we lose as a team," Guy Lauzon said. "We have no room for an independent thinker on our team."

"You're here to be a team player," Larry Miller said, who a few hours earlier had tried to rip apart Chuck Strahl, "and you bet it's a problem if you're not supporting your colleagues. You have to be a team player. If you're not, then get out." Added Jim Flaherty, "You owe a duty to everyone. To the team. The team comes first."

My team at that moment was a pack. In the course of that conversation, and the early-morning Ontario caucus meeting, it became clear the conflict was not over information, but dissension. The caucus, the party, the leader, the PMO all expected unanimity of thought and unity of direction. And while this was understood clearly by an experienced MP and caucus member, it was the first time I'd seen this demand made when MPs were excluded from forming or influencing policy.

On all the substantive issues of 2006—from Afghanistan to same-sex marriage to the green plan to program spending cuts to budget initiatives to pension-splitting to income trust taxation to the Quebecois nation to law and order measures—there were no national caucus debates. MPs were not consulted as policy was being formulated and were told of decisions after they were made and normally after they had been announced to the media. In this environment, the only way possible to catch the attention of ministers and Harper himself was to speak outside of caucus and to use the media. This was exactly my logic behind staging a national conference on pension-splitting after lobbying Jim Flaherty in caucus and not receiving a response. It's why I blogged about climate change measures in advance of the green plan, and family tax reforms in the weeks and months before the 2006 budget.

After all, what was an MP there for—in Ottawa, in the House, in a party, in caucus—if it was not to lobby for the hopes, dreams, and agenda items of the people who sent him there? Was the job of an MP to support the party and the caucus and the leader? Or was it to work for the voters back home? How could a truly effective MP be a part of, and subjugated within, a team that did not listen, and did not care to?

Mostly, though, my colleagues feared me. Some were afraid my renegade ways and media profile would make them look ineffective to voters. Some feared I would hurt the team by questioning its monolithic, undebated policy positions. All were terrified at the power and growing influence of this new form of communication—a digital tide parties could not control, a direct connect between a politician and citizens. Worse, between Garth Turner and their own constituents. The blog scared the hell out of them. They couldn't eliminate it. But they could eliminate me.

This day, of course, settled nothing. But it also ended with an apology.

You have made it much clearer where you believe the line sits, I said. And I will not go near it. You have my word. A few hands were extended as the room emptied. I shook with Daryl Kramp, Larry Miller, then Gord Brown. I left the cabinet area alone, found an empty stairwell off an upper floor of the Centre Block, sat, and shook.

That night I researched Jeff Watson, trying to understand his anger and motivation. In addition to his education and career, I learned he is a man of deep faith who opposes abortion and same-sex marriage, who has four children, and who was an orphan. The next day during QP I sent him a note, apologizing for my joking remark in Cornwall about his parents. He responded:

Garth—thank you for the apology regarding my parents. Most people have the great opportunity to have two parents to love, some have only one, and others, sadly none. I was blessed with two sets of parents, one who gave me life, the other great opportunity. We, in turn, are beginning the process of adopting an orphaned baby girl from China. All my best, Jeff.

It was gracious. I was disarmed. And, sadly, I never saw it coming.

On Monday, October 17, 2006, newly elected Green Party leader Elizabeth May arrived in the foyer of the House of Commons for a webcast interview that I'd post on my blog after QP. It was the first time I'd met the woman, and the encounter had been lined up by my staffer. May was a gregarious, charming, and politically aggressive woman. She made the most of my bringing her into that frenetic space by darting off to talk to Lib environment critic John Godfrey and then trolling for microphones.

The interview was welcomed, since we were just a few days away from the unveiling of the Conservatives' long-awaited green plan, and I'd been lobbying for substantial climate change initiatives. Little did I realize how many eyes were upon the two of us in that crowded space as we stood before my assistant with his digital camera and wrist-mounted hard drive.

The next day, just twenty-four hours in advance of Minister Rona Ambrose tabling her strategy—quickly shredded by every credible environmentalist—I blogged:

The debate about whether global warming is a crock or a catastrophe will get steamier this week as the Harper Administration unveils its long-awaited green plan. I cannot tell you tonight exactly when that will be, but Rona Ambrose's office told mine earlier today there will be a lock-up in advance of the release.

So, it's coming. And today in Question Period two of the players in this enviro-drama sat about fifty feet from each other, but directly in their mutual line of vision. On the floor of the House of Commons was Ambrose the environment minister, who the opposition pilloried for months, thinking she was an attractive Alberta lightweight they could trample. But Ambrose, so far at least, has stood her ground like a linebacker and gained a big following within the Conservative caucus.

Above her and looking on from the public gallery was Elizabeth May, the leader of the Green Party. Unlike the petite, angular, cool, brunette, and impeccable Ambrose, May exudes an earth-motherliness punctuated by flying blonde hair, black glasses, an uninhibited laugh, and lots of touching. It's an interesting study in contrasts. Does it set the scene for conflict?

May insists no, as I bring her into the foyer of the House—forbidden territory, since she is not an elected MP—for an interview with MPtv. She says she'd be only too happy to congratulate Ambrose on a knock-out climate change strategy document, but quickly adds that she doesn't expect to be doing so. I find the woman to be sharp, engaging, and surprisingly political, weaving in anti-Conservative messages that seem to go deep beyond the environmental file. She's also a networker, taking full advantage of my delivering her to this sacred spot to buttonhole Liberal environment critic John Godfrey and try to catch the eye of some of the media gods.

May is clearly frustrated that while she leads a national party with federal funding and candidates in every riding, she likely will not be part of any leaders' debate in the next election or, for that matter, be taken seriously enough by these reporters milling around.

So, this week is as crucial to her as it is to Ambrose. The stakes are enormous for both of them, just as they are for Canadians.

As I have stated, climate change is a defining issue, and this is a landmark time for a generational government. Either we will rise to the challenge, or we will not. Those scribes sitting in the lockup will be reading about mandatory emission levels, permission-based production, mandated clean air, water, and renewable energy targets, the fostering of green technology, and a strategy of sustainable development, or they'll read about voluntary targets, an absolute increase in greenhouse gases, the economic supremacy of the oil sands, and industry consultations.

A new green plan was not one of the government's vaunted five priorities. It was not even a campaign promise, with the environment relegated to a trashing of Kyoto and a practical tax credit to get people on the train and the bus. But in politics a week's a long time and eight months is almost a life. Now global warming is household stuff. An administration born of tax cuts and tough-love crime bills must react with conviction.

Unexpected, perhaps, but utterly unavoidable. And a moment now looking for a heroine.

It did not occur to me, perhaps naively, how seriously the May encounter, the blog entry, and PMO concern about the coming Clean Air Act would be taken together. That would soon change.

Wednesday morning's Ontario caucus meeting was routine and unmemorable until 8:45 a.m. when I became aware that Jeff Watson had once again taken the microphone. What he said was no less shocking the second time, but now it was to be followed by a staccato series of events that would take just thirteen minutes.

"I move that Garth Turner be removed from this caucus," Watson said. This time he did not allege a security breach. In fact, the words "caucus confidentiality" were not spoken by anyone until more than three hours later when national caucus chair Rahim Jaffer spat them out them during a frenzied media scrum.

In moments, Gary Goodyear and Scott Reid were lined up to speak. Both had in their hands reprints of blog postings. Both their sheaves were stapled in the corners and highlighted in yellow. Goodyear, a professional chiropractor—first elected in 2004 by just over two hundred votes—was Harper's choice for Ontario caucus chair prior to Brown. An anti-gay-marriage crusader, he was endorsed in the 2006 campaign by Vote Marriage Canada, and won by almost six thousand votes over Liberal and welder Janko Peric. "Canada can rest," he said on election night, "we have ended a regime of corruption."

On this morning he also spoke passionately. He quoted from the blog entry above, emphasizing my description of May, quoting my concerns about Harper's coming climate change plan, and then shoved his papers over his head and asked, "Is Garth setting himself up so if the green plan does not meet his expectations he will embarrass this party and this caucus?"

I would find out later that day, at 6 p.m., from *The Star*'s Susan Delacourt (who was smoking a cigarette outside the National Press Building) that some caucus members were telling reporters Garth Turner had been planning a defection to the Green Party the next day, in protest of Ambrose's tepid Clean Air Act. "So, are you going to do it?" she asked. And I told her, truthfully, that I'd met Elizabeth May for the first time two days earlier, for fifteen minutes, had not spoken to her since, and never planned to go Green. But, a few minutes after giving a media conference I could not have imagined in my wildest dreams, I wasn't ruling anything out. "Too bad," she said. "I think you should do it."

The next morning, Ms. Delacourt's story, splashed across the front page of the *Toronto Star*, read:

Could Garth Turner, the ejected Conservative from Halton, be the first Green Party MP in the House of Commons? Green leader Elizabeth May told the Toronto Star she is "absolutely" ready to make the invitation and Turner, interviewed yesterday, says he might be interested, after he's talked to his constituents about his abrupt ouster from Conservative ranks.

If Turner does go Green, Prime Minister Stephen Harper could find that a simple fact of caucus discipline, as it was billed, could alter the Canadian political landscape.

Harper isn't expected to give environmentalists much to praise when he unveils his big green-plan announcement today, but he may have handed the Green Party an unintentional gift nevertheless. One Green Party MP in the Commons is all it takes to move the party into the next election debates and into greater prominence at the daily scrums after question period.

"Obviously, we'd welcome him with arms wide open," May said last night.

It's not an ideological stretch for Turner, May noted, citing the Halton MP's position as a director on the Sierra Legal Defence Fund, as well as Turner's recent Internet postings on the proposed green plan, which he suspects are the real reason behind his ejection from caucus yesterday.

Scott Reid took over now and referenced a half dozen blog references from the papers in his hand to "hats and horses," "social conservatives," and Charles McVety. "Colleagues, we do not need a voice of dissension from within," the MP said, to a smatter of applause. Moments before, there had been none. Unlike the first assault a month less a day earlier, when the Watson motion seemed to surprise all but a few caucus members, this time there was a growing unanimity, more support, more organization, more preparation and involvement.

With each moment, momentum was gaining. I watched quietly,

took notes, tried to see what was happening more as a news event than an execution.

Guy Lauzon was next, giving a version of the "there is no 'I' in team" speech he'd delivered to me as we sat behind the curtains one day a week earlier, as he asked why in the world anyone would ever interview an NDP member for a webcast. The subject had been BC MP Dawn Black, one of the most experienced members in the Commons. That conversation ended with him calling me a fool, telling me I had to decide "whether I was on the blue team or not." "Guy," I said, "grow up." He smiled curiously and slapped me on the knee.

Lauzon was deputy whip to Jay Hill; he had been a twenty-two-year career civil servant, then soybean plant manager and flea market founder, then failed Alliance candidate, before being elected in 2004 and again in January 2006. Before the 2006 vote, he took heat for going to funerals in the Cornwall area and campaigning. A devout Christian, he'd said in the Commons that giving gays and lesbians the right to marry "is like saying that all men should have the right to be mothers." In December 2006, he told the *National Post*, "What my faith helps me with is putting things in perspective and looking at things less selfishly, more globally."

Senator Marjory LeBreton was a surprise participant, after I'd approached her months earlier asking for advice on how to improve relations with Harper. We'd spent time in that big office of hers, looked at the doll she kept sitting on her couch, talking about the Mulroney days, and she told me just to give it all time. "You're a very talented person," she said, "and this leader will come to see that more and more."

"What Garth has to learn," she told the room now, "is that you've got to support the prime minister, absolutely no matter what." LeBreton had been a Harper opponent when he was Alliance leader and Joe Clark headed the PCs, warning against the potential abandoning of Progressive Conservative values by the socons in any uniting of the right. Then she changed her mind, joined Harper on the campaign bus, moderated his image, and in a few minutes—when national caucus convened—would sit on the front riser with the PM, Jay Hill, House Leader Rob Nicholson, and Caucus Chair Rahim Jaffer, since Marjory was now in cabinet and led the Senate.

Then, a genuine disappointment: Michael Chong followed LeBreton, repeating her message. There is no room in this party for differing opinions, he said. Words he surely reconsidered four weeks later.

The most vitriol, by far, came from the wife of Doug Finley, who once again had slipped into the Ontario caucus room—for just the second time since the election. Human Resources minister at the time, Diane Finley took the microphone nearest to where I was sitting and, turning to stare at me through her dark glasses, spoke to me in the third person, called me Belinda Stronach. "This caucus was far, far better off when that woman left this room," she said, "and we will be better off when this one is gone."

Helena Guergis was on her feet, accusing me of siphoning off support in her riding by catering to seniors' groups over pension-splitting. "Garth Turner should be ashamed of himself," she said.

Twelve days after my ouster, Guergis would issue a media release, headed "Simcoe-Grey's MP Helena Guergis Successful with Income-Splitting." In it she said, "Our seniors, who have contributed their lives to building Canada as we know it, today are to be commended in working with me on this very important development." Ever flamboyant, Helena left her bed and bath gift shop business in the Rainbow Mall in Angus, Ontario, to work in the riding office of an Ontario MPP. A beauty queen, she won the title of "Miss Huronia" then competed for "Miss Oktoberfest" and in the Canadian search for "Miss Universe." She then served as an advisor to Ontario education minister Janet Ecker, lost a 2003 bid to be an MPP, and in 2004, won her federal seat with a hundred-vote margin.

In 2003, Guergis campaigned as being in favour of same-sex

marriage. In 2004, she campaigned in opposition to it, and voted against Bill c-38 in 2005. That same year she tabled a private member's bill that would force any MP switching parties to run in a by-election within thirty-five days. "It's about democracy, it's about integrity and restoring voter confidence," she said at the time. "Canadians have become cynical of politicians who turn on a dime and switch their political allegiance."

On February 8, 2006, Guergis informed the media she would issue a press release reaffirming her support for anti-floor-crossing legislation. The next day, David Emerson—elected on January 23 as a Liberal—was appointed to the cabinet as minister for international trade, and Stephen Harper made Helena Guergis Mr. Emerson's parliamentary secretary. Her news release was never issued. On January 4, 2007, Ms. Guergis would become the Honourable Helena Guergis, as she was sworn into Stephen Harper's cabinet as the secretary of state for Foreign Affairs, International Trade, and Sport.

It was nearing nine o'clock, and Gord Brown stepped down from the podium in a dramatic and telling move, walking to a floor mic so he could speak as a caucus member, not chair, to say, "We must put all dissent behind us. We cannot afford to be seen debating these issues and risk being attacked as a result. This has to be put behind us, once and for all. I'm for voting." Any doubt now as to what would happen in a few moments was dispelled.

And then Finance Minister Jim Flaherty got up to speak, and I could not help but remember the February breakfast we shared at the Toronto hotel at Kennedy Road and the 401. He had pumped me about how to set up a GTA caucus, about staff and what to expect on the Hill. I told him about my plans to put together a pre-budget report and involve as many Canadians as possible in the project, and I interviewed him on tape at the table for a podcast broadcast on garth.ca, just after Liberal Jim Karygiannis had come over and asked if I'd be running to be Speaker of the House. Flaherty was forthright, charming, and supportive, and I liked him instantly, even though he left me to pay the bill.

In the caucus room Flaherty referenced my campaign to get income-splitting for retired Canadians. "I don't appreciate Garth Turner pushing things this government has not decided on," he said. "He is not running an alternative government."

But there was some support from among MPs who did not seem to have been briefed. Harold Albrecht, of Kitchener, looked shocked and asked, "Where did all this come from? Was it on the agenda, and if it wasn't then why is this being pushed so hard?"

David Tilson, three-time MP and Orangeville lawyer, stood like an oak in the storm. "We may not like some of what Garth says," he thundered, "but it sure as hell is his right to say it. If we do this thing this morning, it will send out a very negative message, and especially to the media."

The speeches mostly over, the room was in a surly mood, ready to vote. I stood, recognizing the inevitability of what was about to happen, and asked only that a reason be attached to the motion. "Without one, this will not be positive."

To that, Diane Finley, now standing at the back of the room beside her husband, yelled, "Are you threatening us?" In the end, no reason for the action would be given. It certainly, apparently, was not about caucus confidentiality.

They voted by hand—eighteen in favour, six against, a dozen abstainers. The place emptied in an instant save for four or five members, and I sat in my place for lack of anything better to do, absorbing my last few seconds in the caucus room. Dean Del Mastro, the rookie MP for Peterborough whose office was next to mine at Justice, and who served with me on the Finance Committee, came over and shook my hand. "I just wanted you to know that I enjoyed working with you on the committee," he said. And I wondered how he'd know that the next day I'd be relieved of my duties there.

It was nine-fifteen. Members would start to filter in for national caucus in a few minutes. Twenty minutes earlier I was listening to announcements and going over my schedule for the day. Now, moving through the doorway and heading for the Government Lobby, there was a yawning realization, watching Conservative MPs flee in my path, that something far more momentous than having my ass kicked out of regional caucus was taking place.

The speed. The immediate roster of speakers. The prepared blog reprints. Finley's presence. Flaherty's coup de grace. Brown's big move. LeBreton's unusual presence. Reid's highlighter. Del Mastro's comment. It was all there—censure from the PM's chief of political operations, from the second most powerful man in his cabinet, from the government leader in the Senate, from the PM's chosen caucus chair and Harper's personal political organizer, as well as a message from the whip, delivered by his deputy.

And at that moment I did not know that the House IT department had been scheduled to shut down and reconfigure computers in both my Hill and riding offices in three hours, or that the Speaker's office had ordered the printer to run off a new seating plan for the Commons showing me in Seat 279, in the last row in the far corner opposite the government, which would be ready for Question Period that afternoon.

It was only evident that national caucus was about to echo what Ontario caucus had done.

It was nine-eighteen. In the foyer, I passed Julie van Dusen, the CBC reporter whom Stephen Harper a few weeks earlier had openly called a "junk journalist" in caucus. "What's up?" she said as usual, then peering at me over her ever-present notebook, "and what's the matter?"

"Give me a few minutes. I think I'm the story," I said.

She looked at me for an instant. "I'm getting a camera."

The government lobby would be quiet, as caucus members gathered at the other end of the building. There were also phones there, and I needed George. The cell in my pocket was hardly an option.

Four minutes had elapsed since the Ontario caucus ended and nobody from that meeting was in the broad corridor leading from there to the lobby. As the leaded glass and wood door swung open, only Diane Ablonczy was visible, sitting at a round table with her assistant, whom I recognized from Finance Committee meetings.

Ablonczy's credentials as a voice of the West and a Reformer are second to none. She has been continuously elected since 1993; an Alliance leadership candidate; a Western Canada Concept member in the eighties; and an effective, respected performer in the Commons and on committee. Her failure to make it into Harper's cabinet was newsworthy and obviously a critical disappointment but then, as Flaherty's parliamentary secretary, she was included in cabinet-level briefings and spoke confidently for the minister. A teacher and lawyer, she was also open, accessible, and—to me—empathetic as she watched my ongoing struggle within the confines of the neo-Con caucus.

Seeing the opening door, Ablonczy looked up and saw it was me. We'd shared a few private moments together, including in my car as I drove her back to her office one night after dinner at 24 Sussex—my only invitation by the Harpers, on the night of the first pivotal vote to extend the mission in Afghanistan. She talked about her three grand-children and her husband, Ron, struggling to make the farm imple-ment business a success.

Immediately, she mouthed the words, "I'm sorry." I realized she had not been in the meeting.

George didn't pick up, so I left a message. He would call back within five minutes. Diane came over, folded her hands on the back of one of the upholstered chairs beside the whip's desk, and spoke to me without referencing the event that had just taken place and, as was now evident, was on schedule.

"What will you do next?" she asked gently. It could have been a mine for information or it might have been genuine. I sensed compassion, but said it was completely unknown what might happen, other than national caucus was certain to remove me in the next few minutes. She did not comment. The natural reaction would be to attack, she said, but it would be far more constructive "to accept this, and deal with it. There will be a lot of people watching," she said, "and you will not get a second chance."

Second chance? I took that to mean a second chance at first impressions, and I imagined the horde of media that was likely gathering outside, having followed Julie van Dusen's camera. I thanked her for speaking to me, as George called on my BlackBerry. Ablonczy melted off to caucus, and George told me to leave immediately.

"You do not know enough," he said. "Harper has just done the big fuck with you. This is it, pal, so get the fuck out of there. And get off this fucking cellphone!"

Heading out the loading dock doorway, past the smokers, I ran into Paul Martin. As a former prime minister, he got a black sedan, a driver, and a modest RCMP security detail. Every day he was on the Hill, however, he chose to have the car parked in the back, out of sight, beside the foundation stones of the refurbished Library of Parliament. He was consistently charming, dignified, and supportive of me.

We exchanged the usual friendly remarks, and it was natural to wonder how he coped with quickly changed circumstances, from PM to bum to failed party leader, to the back door of Parliament, while upstairs the man who narrowly defeated him exercised utter control and now defined confidence and power. Mr. Harper had swept into power calling Paul Martin corrupt and his party "mafia-like."

Back at the condo I gave Dorothy a quick call at home in Campbellville and asked her not to watch television or listen to the radio. I called George and we spoke for an hour. I called Esther in the riding office at around 10:30. "What is going on?" she yelled at me. "The world is going nuts, it's exploding. There are cameras everywhere. Tell me, tell me!"

Just after noon, I flicked on the TV and viewed live coverage of Rahim Jaffer walking out of the national caucus room that I'd exited three hours earlier. He was about to dishonour me in front of the country, my wife who could not bear to be the last to know, and my staff who were incredulous. At that moment, it occurred to me, I was watching a man who, five years earlier, had sent his parliamentary assistant, Matthew Johnston, to impersonate him on a Vancouver radio station.

The next morning, the *Globe and Mail*'s page one story, "Troubles grip Tories" reported it, in part, this way:

> Conservative national caucus chair Rahim Jaffer said the Ontario Tory caucus passed a unanimous motion to expel Mr. Turner during yesterday morning's meeting. The motion was then approved unanimously by all Tory MPs and senators in the national caucus. MPs felt Mr. Turner was violating caucus confidentiality on his daily weblog, Mr. Jaffer said.
>
> In subsequent days, members of the Halton Conservative electoral district association passed a motion, at a long and stormy meeting attended by Wally Butts, Conservative National Executive Council member Richard Ciano, and Finley assistant Joseph Dow, asking answers to ten questions. One of them was,

"what evidence will be provided substantiating Garth Turner's suspension."

On November 10, the answer would be received. Rahim Jaffer wrote: "There will be no evidence forthcoming; this is an internal caucus matter."

When Wally Butts left that meeting in a room in the Milton Sports Centre he passed by my chair, squeezed my hand, and said, "I am very sorry." He had sad eyes.

At 4 p.m. my assistant Bill Zimmerly and I shot an MPtv video standing in front of the Langevin Block that was posted on garth.ca, and would be downloaded seventy thousand times within the next few hours. That day the website was overwhelmed by hits, and webmaster William Stratas used every means at his disposal to cope with the traffic.

At five there was a media conference in the theatre of the National Press Building that was carried live by most networks, lasted about forty minutes, and in which I felt a sense of detachment. All day media calls had been barraging my Hill office, the riding office, and my cellphone. Television cameras came to shoot B-roll in both offices, and I saw that two more were camped out on Sussex Drive outside my apartment. By the time the conference happened, I felt like the whole thing belonged on *Entertainment Tonight*.

After the conference I did five or six studio interviews, packed up, got in the car, and left Ottawa. On the 401 there were twelve more radio interviews. I got home around midnight, wrote a crucial blog entry, went to bed at two, and got up at four to drive to Toronto for rounds of the morning news shows. Operating on sheer fumes, I was driven to do this. Jaffer had lied. Caucus had been steamrolled. Party was whipping principle.

At eleven we held another media conference, which was intended for local riding newspapers. Instead, about fifty media outlets showed up, and satellite trucks were lined up outside my tiny Main Street riding office. Unbeknownst to me at the time, a neighbour and blogger, Peter Near, was there, and posted this a few hours later:

Today I snuck out of work for an hour to attend the press conference for ousted MP Garth Turner. I consider myself lucky to be close to this historic event in Canadian politics, and wanted to experience it in person.

Today's press conference was held in the local riding office on Main Street in Milton, about 3 minutes from my house, and it was about as much of a zoo as this little town has ever seen. When I arrived, satellite trucks lined the same street where every weekend farmers set up their booths to sell sweet corn and home-made pies. Inside the constituency office the air was damp as it tends to get when you cram too many people into a small space, add studio lighting, and turn up the stress levels to eleven.

The mix was one of reporters and political supporters, as for non-affiliated common folk I bet I was the only one of those in attendance. There was a surprisingly large turnout from the Green Party, including Milton's Green candidate from the last election and several Green supporters sporting Green Party buttons. A few minutes into the press conference there was an older gentleman who couldn't get in and started to make a fuss, he was escorted politely away from the door so that the conference could continue but I felt bad for him because he was obviously passionate about being there and might just have been the number two "average voter" to join me in my pilgrimage.

Garth's statement was not unlike others that he made last night and today on his blog. The reporters in the room were desperately trying to bait him into saying something bad about the prime minister, and he barely took the bait. Lots of talk about options going forward like Green Party, Liberal (?), or independent. His stated feeling is that it is very hard to be effective as an independent so I expect that some sort of affiliation or alignment is coming. This led to my question ...

Being apparently the only voter in the room, I felt obliged to speak my mind somewhat especially given the allusion to alternative political alignment. When all the cameras snapped around into my face I became much less eloquent than I would have liked, but the paraphrase of the question was "I fully support your voters-first approach, but the voters of this riding elected you based on the conservative platform. Albeit we understand that there was a Garth spin on the platform, but that is what we elected you on and what we expect. Will you hold true to that platform?"

His answer was that he is a conservative (note the small c that I've used in that description) and will remain true to those ideals. (If you see any of this on the news, I'm the tall guy in the back who could stand to lose a couple of pounds and wearing a brown leather jacket.)

Speaking as one constituent, I can say that for the most part Garth's stances represent my own. I am fiscally conservative and excited about many of the fiscal policies that this government is bringing in and I applaud the push that Garth is making on income-splitting for families. I am however socially liberal and Garth's leaning supports that, most notably in his support for gay marriage. As far as representing me, he does it and while the demographics of Halton are changing daily with all of this rapid growth I believe that he represents the majority in this riding as well.

I was just on a call with some of my US colleagues and explained to them what had happened and why I thought it was historically significant, it might be useful to explain my feelings here on the blog as well. The ousting of Garth Turner brings blogging as a political tool to the front page of every newspaper in the country. He has been very effective at communicating with his constituents via the blog (and for the older demographic via town hall meetings) and I think that everyone will now take notice of its effects. The news story here is in my opinion the incredible grassroots support that Garth Turner has from his electorate, and that support comes directly from the transparency shown by blogging.

People will take notice, and I think that it will change the face of politics in this country very quickly, definitely in time for the next federal election. That is sweeping change, at an incredibly fast pace, and I think that the events of the last 24 hours will be the catalyst for that change. It will signal a return of democracy to the people and will refocus politicians on the people that they represent. It is in my opinion truly historic, and I for one will be proud to tell my grandchildren that I was there when it happened.

It was said in my dealings with the media and the Canadians who flooded in to comment—four hundred blog postings, 1,200 emails, and countless phone calls in a few hours—that it was difficult to see who benefited from the events of that day. Caucus looked extreme, then manipulated. The prime minister looked like a control freak. The party looked like it could not tolerate dissent. Garth Turner looked like a verbose gadfly. Parliament looked dysfunctional, and the green plan, extreme in its importance, did not even top the news cycle when it was unveiled the next day. Around the world the story made headlines for just one reason—I was one of the first politicians ever to lose his job for blogging.

Some would say the journey embarked upon when I decided not to lie about my feelings on the Emerson appointment led straight to seeing myself getting fired on television eight months later. After all, what party would tolerate such insolence? Countless Conservatives blamed me for damaging the first hopeful leader the country had chosen in thirteen years. The blogosphere was choked with posters arguing I was being vindictive for not having been selected for Harper's cabinet. Others just dismissed the member from Halton as a media hog and a headline whore, incapable of doing or saying anything that did not deliberately draw attention. Others asked, simply, did you not know what kind of a person Stephen Harper was before you stuck his logo on your election sign?

As an independent, outside the caucus and suddenly divorced from the party that had defined my entire political life, as well as that of my family, all of these comments hurt. But, through it all, it was still impossible to see who benefited. Certainly not the voters.

Since making the first decision forced upon me by "Emerson," I'd elected to put principle before party. Since being told by the prime minister that truth-telling journalists made bad politicians, I'd chosen to prove him wrong. Since being ordered by staffer Brodie to stop talking to the media and issue a statement I could not agree with, I vowed to never do either. Since being set up by Finley for sacrifice to a televangelist, I'd sworn to defend moderation. Since being disenfranchised by unaccountable party backroomers, I'd embraced digital democracy.

And now, since being thrown out of my own party, I knew. Men create parties. Principles create men.

"I've got spies everywhere."

—Doug Finley, director of political operations, Conservative Party

JUST BEFORE SIX on the evening of Wednesday, May 31, 2006, Martin O'Hanlon, Ottawa news editor of the Canadian Press, sent me an email:

We just got this news release. Any idea if the PMO put these guys up to it? I'm asking off the record—we're not planning a story.

Attached was a media release O'Hanlon would not take seriously, issued by a group called the Institute for Canadian Values, and listing as contact person Joseph Ben-Ami, who would turn out to be an orthodox Jew closely associated with an anti-gay group called Defend Marriage Canada.

Under the headline, "Institute for Canadian Values calls on Harper to discipline MP Garth Turner for bigoted comments," Ben-Ami released what appeared to be a work of fiction by a band of religious zealots, so far off mainstream thought that O'Hanlon and every other news organization in the country dismissed it.

"Last week Garth Turner attacked so-called 'ethnics' on television, complaining about their impact on nomination meetings for political parties," said Joseph Ben-Ami, Executive Director of the Institute of Canadian Values. "Now he is targeting people of faith on his blog, especially those who support the traditional definition of marriage, calling them 'taliban' and accusing them of an 'agenda of hate.'

87

"Grossly ignorant and bigoted comments such as these are unacceptable in any civilized society, especially a multicultural one like Canada, and Turner should be held accountable for them."

Turner's ethnic comments were made during a televised debate last Friday on the CHTV station in Hamilton.

"When Garth Turner arranges to bring his family and friends to a nomination meeting on a bus he calls it democracy, but when a challenger who happens to be brown-skinned, or perhaps a member of the local church or synagogue, does the same thing for their family and friends, he calls them Taliban and accuses them of 'taking over,'" observed Ben-Ami. "It's actually quite pathetic."

"Garth Turner's behaviour is a sharp illustration of the vicious and deep-rooted bigotry lurking just below the surface of the secular left in our society," continued Ben-Ami. "People like him claim to be champions of tolerance, but when their own ideas and positions are challenged, they resort to name-calling and fear mongering, laughably invoking the principle of tolerance to justify their bigotry. What really shocks is that so many are gullible enough to believe them."

That night an online petition, addressed to Stephen Harper, appeared on the website of the Christian news service, word.ca, asking for Garth Turner's removal from the Conservative caucus. It included Stephen Harper's fax and phone numbers, email, and street address at the Langevin Block.

The site, word.ca, features on its homepage graphic a picture of Stockwell Day, the Security Minister in Stephen Harper's government, and the man Mr. Harper defeated to become the leader of the Canadian Alliance Party. The Alliance merged with the Progressive Conservatives in 2003 to become the Conservative Party of Canada. Joseph

Ben-Ami was a consultant to Day when he was leader of the official opposition, and was director of operations for Stockwell's 2002 leadership campaign. Following this, Mr. Ben-Ami became chief lobbyist for B'nai Brith Canada in Ottawa, as that organization's director of communications.

On June 6, Ben-Ami wrote a column, "Commentary on MP Garth Turner," which was distributed electronically to the offices of all 308 members of Parliament, and posted widely on Internet Christian sites. In it, he claimed to have worked on my 1993 leadership campaign for the Progressive Conservative party (there is no record of that), which was won by Kim Campbell, and said, "I have been active in Conservative politics for the last thirty years, longer, I suspect, than almost all of those who voted for Mr. Turner in his last nomination meeting."

The column attacked comments I'd made about Ben-Ami's colleague, Charles McVety, during a televised debate a couple of weeks earlier, likened me to those bigoted against blacks and Jews, and quoted this from a poem by German theologian Martin Niemoller on the Nazis: "When they came for the Jews I did not speak out for I was not a Jew. When they came for me, there was no one left to speak out."

Mr. Ben-Ami concluded thusly:

To be sure, Garth Turner and his ready-made audience are not Nazis, not even close. But the ease with which they ridicule their fellow Canadians who happen to be Christian is disquieting to say the least, as is the obvious and perverse pleasure they all seem to derive from the offence they are causing.

As a Jew, I will not be silent, because if I'm silent when Christians are the target, who will be there when the focus shifts to me? Garth Turner??

On June 8, my office started receiving the first of many emails with the subject line, "Renegade Conservative MP Garth Turner calls

Ethnic and Religious People Flowers of Evil and Taliban."

On June 9, an extensive article was published on the widely read Christian website LifeSiteNews.com, referencing the television debate between McVety and myself on May 28, saying, "It came to the fore that one of the goals of Christian political activists is to work to ensure that anti-marriage, anti-life, anti-Christian Conservative MPs are defeated and replaced with more family-friendly and Christian candidates during the nomination meetings that will occur before the next election."

At that time, however, it had not been detailed to members of Stephen Harper's Conservative caucus how, or when, sitting MPs would be required to go through a formal, open, and competitive nomination process. That information was not confirmed until the summer caucus meeting in Cornwall almost a month later, on Friday, August 4, by Doug Finley.

The LifeSiteNews.com article continued, in part:

> Jim Hughes, president of Campaign Life Coalition, a group that works to help elect pro-life candidates, said of Turner, "We said from the beginning that Garth Turner wasn't somebody that could be supported. A lot of people said we just have to vote Conservative regardless of the candidates. And here we're paying the price."
>
> Hughes continued, saying, "The Prime Minister has had this man in already and told him to clam up. Now the only thing is for his expulsion from Cabinet [sic]. That would satisfy the bulk of people who supported Mr. Harper from the life and family movement."

On June 22, the possibility of pro-family, pro-life, Christian supporters of Mr. Harper targeting the nomination meetings and political survival of certain Conservative MPs was the subject of an article in Toronto's *NOW* magazine. Looking forward to the same-sex vote, which was held in Parliament in December 2006, Jill Cahoon of the Alberta-based United Families Canada, a member group of McVety's Defend Marriage Canada, said, "We will be looking at the vote.... We will encourage people to get involved politically when nominations take place for the next election."

On June 13, commenting on the rapid events of the past few weeks, the moderate Christian website, Bene Diction Blogs On, posted these observations:

> Garth Turner made a fundamental mistake when he attempted to argue and reason with Charles McVety on a recent TV appearance. The fallout was swift and Turner was the subject of attack from this single-issue, religious Right group led by Dr. Charles McVety called Institute for Canadian Values, and who is involved in Canadian Christian College and Christian Coalition International Canada. Turner was not surprised finding himself targeted in Lifesite News (Canada–US religious news site) by emailers, and McVety had his group email every federal conservative MP as well as the PM.
>
> Joseph C. Ben-Ami, of the Institute for Canadian Values who is also attacking Turner, attended the War on Christian Conference in Washington, held by Vision America, a well-known religious Right restoration group.
>
> Turner was the only Conservative MP to stand by Saskatchewan Christian fundamentalist MP Maurice Vellacott recently when Vellacott made more of his famous, inflammatory, inappropriate public remarks ....
>
> My advice to Garth Turner. Don't allow McVety and his ilk to prompt you into public anger. They are trained masters at attack. .. and opportunism.... They've gotten a lot of mileage out of the TV appearance and anger and defense by their perceived opponent only feeds their agenda ... that Canadian Christians are under

persecution. They are superspiritual—single-issue groups operating under the Christian faith. They are not representative of the vast majority of evangelicals in Canada and they do not represent us.

But, apparently, Charles McVety was influential within the Stephen Harper caucus and, according to Mr. McVety, the prime minister's office itself.

In April of 2005 the Canadian Real Estate Association asked me to deliver a keynote address at the annual convention on the restoration of property rights. There was a great view of Parliament Hill from the hotel room window and I decided then that I would seek to return as an MP after leaving this cold city in 1993 as the Jean Chretien tide swept in.

My old riding had been carved up and I chose to run in the populous southern hunk, now called Halton. There were already three people in the race, but the only one with federal election experience was D'Arcy Keene, who had run for the Progressive Conservatives in Scarborough in 1993, where he was pummelled by John MacKay. Keene, I was told, was being backed by GTA-area Conservative MP Peter van Loan, now Stephen Harper's House Leader, and their mutual friend and national party director, Richard Ciano. In fact, Ciano uncharacteristically showed up at the monthly meeting of the Halton Conservative Electoral District Association (EDA) at which both Keene and I declared our intention to seek the nomination. It was the only time he would appear at such a meeting until the one after I was removed from caucus. By late 2006, Ciano sat on the National Council meeting of the party, and helped make two decisions which could not be appealed—to set aside my nomination as a CPC candidate in the next federal election, and to disqualify me from ever running again as a Conservative. Anywhere.

Ciano had been president of van Loan's riding association, and he claims on his website to be responsible for the MP's win in the 2004 federal election. Richard Ciano previously served in Mike Harris's Queen's Park administration, as a staffer with MPP Derwyn Shea and cabinet minister Al Palladini. Van Loan was also a long-time Tory backroom force, serving as president of the Ontario wing of the party from 1994 to 1998, where he took partial credit for Mike Harris forming a government, then as national president until he resigned over a bitter and public disagreement with leader Joe Clark. Van Loan tried to recruit first New Brunswick premier Bernard Lord to run as leader, then Nova Scotia MP Peter MacKay. He afterwards ran the successful national "Yes" campaign to have the Progressive Conservatives merge with Stephen Harper's Canadian Alliance, before being elected to represent York-Simcoe.

In the 2005 Halton nomination, Keene lost. It was evident to us from the get-go that he would fail, and by exactly the huge amount we calculated. Despite that, he seemed crushed on the night of the decision—shocked and disbelieving. He had engineered a massive entry into the nomination hall, complete with flag bearers, bagpipers, and processionaries, almost comical in its excess for a candidate who would finish third of four.

However, nomination night was consistent with his behaviour during the campaign itself, which was extremely cocksure and aggressive. While I worked the phones night and day, churning through hundreds of party members, Keene would do the unlikely, and show up unannounced at people's homes and spend long hours lobbying them. It was obvious the technique was time-consuming, inefficient, and bound to fail. He was an experienced operative and party executive, and it was evident he must have had another, parallel, strategy—something that made him confident he would emerge victorious.

I would not know what that was until more than a year later. It was televangelist and self-avowed Harper insider, Charles McVety.

The massive CH television building in downtown Hamilton is charming for many reasons. Its modernistic steel exterior, a visual reminder of the city's industrial heritage, is glued into the back of a nineteenth-century stone mansion. The main entrance has evolved to be a questionable staircase beside the rear loading dock. And inside the back door are reprints of fifty-year-old stories from *The Hamilton Spectator* that document testing of the station's first transmitting antenna. "First Signal sent out by CHCH, Preparatory to Opening Monday," said *The Spec* on June 4, 1954. That's when everyone believed television would change everything.

I arrived late for the interview, having just done battle with a class of Grade 10 girls who were convinced the Conservative immigration practices were barbaric. The topic Esther had agreed to for CH, now a part of the Global empire after four decades of independence, was "Harper vs. the Media," but once the lights went up and the VTR rolled, it turned out to be about gay marriage and the RCMP. It was a complete surprise to me, which made me wonder if the producer, Lawrence Diskin, knew he'd never get me on the show to discuss the same-sex issue.

In a moment I was doing a double-ender with a guy I'd never heard of before who was obviously a religious leader opposed to gay marriage. He sounded like a wingnut, so debating him ended up being amusing, almost fun. Then he switched horses and spoke of defeating MPs who disagreed with his homophobic view by encouraging people of faith to stack nomination meetings. So we clashed, and I expressed my view that nominations that are hijacked by single-interest groups—whether that involves church members or busloads of people who represent one cultural or ethnic group—do not serve democracy well. Candidates can become one-trick ponies, installed for narrow reason, and be completely unreflective of the community at large. Any party that lets that happen jeopardizes both the political system and its own chances of success.

My opponent, Charles McVety, immediately called me a racist and anti-Christian.

"That was fun," co-host Donna Skelly said when the tape stopped, as Lawrence sheepishly came out of the control room. Who was that guy? I asked, and was told he headed Defend Marriage Canada and was on the show because he'd targeted several Conservative MPs in favour of same-sex marriage, including James Moore of BC and Nova Scotia's Gerald Keddy. It made for good TV.

That night my blog read, in part:

> As you might discern, I have no time for groups in our society who try to force their morals, or their culture, on the rest of us. This is not "direct democracy" but rather a plucking of the political system's most fragile flower—the nomination meeting. In almost any riding in Canada, on any night of a nomination meeting, the arrival of 400 or 500 card-carrying insta-members will elect you a golden retriever, if that's want they want. It is the antithesis of democracy in a country where 1% of us belong to political parties and the other 99% trust us to get it right.
>
> Faith-based politics is fine. It has a long tradition. It can accomplish a lot of good. But when one religious or cultural group engineers a coup, overwhelming existing political party members and workers, and replacing a politician elected by a plurality of people with a single-issue monochromatic militant, well, kiss democracy goodbye.

Then, to emphasize the point that a political administration based entirely on a faith agenda, as Defend Marriage Canada and McVety were suggesting, would not work—and had failed elsewhere —these words were added. I would soon realize how provocative they were.

Call it Defend Marriage Canada. Call it the Taliban. Fleurs du mal.

A fundamental rule of combat is to know your enemy, know his skills. But an even more basic rule is to know when you have one. And in the last week of May 2006, my ignorance of Charles McVety surely accelerated a chain of events that would lead to my party, or what my party had become, rejecting me as a threat from within.

Where I perceived a pompous, media-loving, homophobic, marginal figure on the fringes of the political landscape, others saw a potent political force with the ability to crown electoral kings. McVety was a man of many hats. He was president of the ten thousand-member Canada Family Action Coalition, with a mandate to "restore Judeo-Christian moral principles in Canada." He was also president and founder of Defend Marriage Canada, an umbrella body representing thirteen groups, including REAL Women—now a familiar lobby group in Harper's Ottawa, whose principal, Gwen Landolt, was a guest at a Conservative function attended by Jason Kenney on the day of the Throne Speech—and the powerful anti-abortion force, Campaign Life.

In 2005 McVety had created the Ottawa-based Institute for Canadian Values which, on the day I was ousted from the Stephen Harper caucus, would issue a media release calling it "a welcome development" less than fifteen minutes after Rahim Jaffer informed the media. "We have long complained about Mr. Turner's conduct in the past, and although, of course, we are not privy to the specific reasons why his colleagues took the action they did today, whatever the reasons, we believe that the action was positive."

Charles McVety installed Joseph Ben-Ami, Stockwell Day's former organizer, and a vocal advocate of Stephen Harper's new childcare allowance, as institute executive director. Both men are stridently anti-abortion, as they are anti-gay. "Abortion," Mr. Ben-Ami told Scott Stinson of the *National Post*, "is largely portrayed as a settled issue in this country, but poll after poll shows the majority of Canadians don't support the position we have in Canada today, which is to say no regulation whatsoever. It's not on their radar screens, because it doesn't affect most Canadians on a daily basis, but sometimes we make the mistake of assuming that because an issue isn't at the top of most Canadians' agendas, we don't want anyone doing anything about it."

Mr. McVety was also the head of the Toronto-based, 1,200-student Canada Christian College, which evolved from the Richmond College bible school founded by his evangelist father, Elmer, forty years ago, and purchased by Charles McVety from his father's estate for $2.1 million.

The college ran afoul of the Ontario government, which revoked its degree-granting privileges. They were restored in 1999 by the Mike Harris government apparently through the efforts of cabinet minister and former Baptist minister Frank Klees, to whose re-election campaign McVety later donated $100,000. In May of 2004, McVety intervened in the Ontario Conservative leadership campaign, instructing party members to vote for Frank Klees or Jim Flaherty against John Tory, in a memo headed "How to Vote to Protect Marriage."

McVety is a broadcaster, host, and owner of Word.ca, a weekly television newsmagazine, seen on Sundays on CTS and Miracle Channel. Stockwell Day was a featured guest, speaking on the "National Marriage Caucus," which McVety organized on Parliament Hill, October 24, 2006, and which was attended by dozens of Conservative MPS. According to Toronto journalist Marci McDonald, in the summer of 2006 McVety also arranged an honorary degree for Stockwell Day from Russia's St. Petersburg State University.

On his television show, Mr. McVety often interviews Joseph Ben-Ami, as well as Rondo Thomas, vice-president of Canada Christian College and the man Charles McVety assisted into the federal Conservative nomination in the riding of Ajax-Pickering prior to the January 2006 election. He ended up being supported by 17,000 voters and won 32 percent of the vote, but lost to Liberal Mark Holland.

Dr. McVety was also a regular weekly commentator on Toronto

radio station AM640 and has turned into a reliable and often-quoted media personality since the January 2006 election. He was the House of Commons VIP gallery guest of federal Finance Minister Jim Flaherty for the reading of the first Harper budget in April 2006. McVety has also made a habit of purchasing many websites using the names of those politicians whom he believes oppose his views, including josephvolpe.com and garthturner.ca (which he linked through to www.garth.ca).

In December of 2005, in the heat of the election campaign, Charles McVety and David Mainse, founder of the nation's leading Christian talk show *100 Huntley Street*, showed up at a Toronto-area rally for Stephen Harper. The *Globe and Mail* reported: "On Saturday, Charles McVety, the Canada Christian College head who also led the Defend Marriage organization against same-sex marriage, turned up at Mr. Harper's Mississauga rally, and was ushered into an office afterward to meet the party leader. But Tory campaign aides again pushed reporters to leave before Mr. McVety had departed."

On the set of the Michael Coren show in the summer of 2006, during a break in an hour-long televised debate with him, Charles McVety bragged that he could "pick up the phone and reach Stephen Harper in two minutes," while it would take me "a month" to do the same. I related that comment to the editors of Canadian Press during an interview in November 2006, and it was subsequently published. McVety immediately issued a press release denying having said it.

But he did. The comment at first struck me as extreme, but no longer. Charles McVety today has his fingers on the pulse of national politics and, as I was to discover during the summer of 2006, is a force within the Conservative Party of Canada itself.

However, on the evening of May 31, when Martin O'Hanlon sent his note, and when I first spoke with the Rev. Charles McVety, I did not know these things. At that time it was not clear that seventy of my 123 caucus colleagues were so-called social conservatives or theo-cons. I did not know there was a caucus bible study session held each Thursday on Parliament Hill. Nor had it been widely broadcast that David Mainse had declared, "We've got a born-again prime minister."

"My fight," McVety said to me, "is with those people who support making prostitution legal, and drugs and legalized marijuana, and who are changing the definition of marriage." He made it clear he spoke of members of Parliament, and the conversation quickly moved to the process Canadians use to choose their MP candidates.

"To me it is a tragedy that less than 1 percent of Canadians actually get involved in this process," he said. "The whole process of nomination is for people to get out and vote and support people who reflect themselves. Garth Turner was not apolitical when he ran for nomination. He was not a sponge that just soaked up people's views. You stood for something."

He spoke at length about my blog. "The messaging from your article was that we, on the other hand, represent just a tiny amount of people, and that we should be compared, as a result, to some kind of evil."

At that point McVety told me I used to be his MP, since he'd lived in North Oakville. He also said he had been behind the candidacy of one of my nomination rivals, D'Arcy Keene. "Yes, I was involved with him," he said. "And there is no room now for the kind of attack you have made. I do not respect name-calling."

Then, "This is not a fight I wish to engage in. I will debate you, but I do not wish to fight you."

But McVety was not finished yet. He signed off by telling me about his deputy, Rondo Thomas, and his run for the Conservative nomination in Ajax-Pickering, which had been successful against an experienced former Tory MP and my old colleague, René Soetens. He said we need more good government, and "we also need ten thousand people at your nomination meeting."

Ralph Reed is an organizer for US evangelical leader Pat Robertson who was invited by Charles McVety to the Canada Christian College to launch the Institute for Canadian Values in early 2006. Among the guests at the sold-out gala dinner, the day after the Canadian federal election, were Jim Flaherty and Conservative senator Anne Cools, who would later also be ejected from the Conservative caucus.

Part of Reed's message was how easily Christian activists can take over the nomination meetings of federal MP candidates. As McVety told journalist Marci McDonald in a mid-2006 interview, "He taught us all that only a handful of people actually go and seriously volunteer to get someone elected. We're talking about 150 people per riding. Tiny numbers! This is the size of a small church."

Added McDonald: "McVety has vowed to wrest Conservative nominations from candidates reluctant to vote out same-sex marriage legislation. One sure target: maverick Conservative Garth Turner, who compared McVety's nomination threat to the modus operandi of the Taliban."

Scott Nicholl stomped into the campaign office shortly after dark, completely pumped. He and his sign crew had been out for hours, apparently playing cat and mouse with the Burlington bylaw enforcement officer. With one of the most severely restrictive sign codes in the country, the city of Burlington—half of which lies inside the federal riding of Halton—prohibits signs on public property, including roadways. That meant that to catch the exodus of Christmas shoppers from area malls, and yet to avoid capture and confiscation, our election posters had to be nailed in, then torn down and moved, and nailed in again, in a rolling pattern, staying one step ahead of the law.

"Hooo-eee," Scott whooped as he joined the strategy meeting, letting in a blast of December air, "we kicked ser-e-ous ass." As it turned out, our sign crews—led by Scott in the crucial urban area—dominated the competition and, in a riding where everyone goes everywhere by car, helped immensely to put the Garth Turner campaign over the top on the night of January 23.

He was a newcomer in his mid-forties, strapping, boisterous, and small-c conservative to the core, and we were happy to have him. Over the months after the election, Scott integrated into the riding association until he was a director, and became one of the five people I completely trusted.

At nine o'clock on the night of August 14, the phone rang in Scott's suburban home. He answered, and at first thought it was a telemarketer calling to suck away more of his money for the federal Tories. "I'm Shannon," the young woman said, "and I am calling on behalf of the Conservative Party of Canada." As Scott was about to hang up on the pitch for a donation, he heard my name. "People in the leadership of the party are not happy with the way Garth Turner has been speaking out," he recalled her saying, "and wish to gain an understanding of how the membership in Halton feels about him."

Scott was all ears now. He was then invited to one of two meetings, "to review Garth Turner's candidacy," the first taking place the next night in Milton. He started to ask questions, at which point the woman passed him over to a man who said he was "in from Ottawa." Are you representing the religious Right wing of the party? Nicholl asked, to which the answer was, "Oh, yes."

At eleven that night, Esther sent out an urgent email to executive members of the Conservative riding association. "You may have heard by now," she said, "the likelihood of a nomination challenge is fast becoming a reality." She included a one-page memo of emergency actions everyone was to start taking the following morning, including an instant membership drive, help with a mass mailing and emailing and, of course, crashing the interlopers' organizational meeting Tuesday night.

About the same time, I posted an article on the blog, which read, in part:

> Depending on what happens over the next couple of days, I may be coming face-to-face with a moral brigade determined to unhorse me and steal away the Conservative Party nomination in Halton that I won in a battle just sixteen months ago. In fact, Scott tells me his caller mentioned the righteous Right folk will be backing one of the guys I defeated.
>
> In case you missed a previous post, the Tory party recently decided not to protect incumbent MPs, the way the Liberals do, but to make them run for their own jobs. The party further decided to take over the local nomination process, deciding when ridings would be "released" to have nominations, and when nomination meetings would be held. So, local party volunteers and workers do not have a role in any of this, and they were as surprised as anyone else last Friday afternoon when the Ottawa headquarters called all Conservative members in Halton and told them the nomination process had begun. (I received an earlier heads-up this might happen.)
>
> I wrote here a few months ago about the threats made by Charles McVety and his moral, anti-gay-marriage crusaders, who made it clear they would target and defeat Tory MPs who do not support opening a national debate on the definition of marriage. I took on McVety and his ilk, calling them intolerant, and stating my view that those who seek to gain political office for religious goals are a danger to our society.
>
> After all, is this piety-in-office belief not at the root of the Islamic fundamentalism and extremism we are fighting in Afghanistan, which Israel has been defending itself against, and

which this week caused a new terror alert paralyzing global air travel? Does Canada's secular and multi-hued, multi-belief society need a dose of literalist religious guidance?

Hey, maybe by making noises about stealing my job at a bussed-in nomination event stacked with insta-Tories, this bunch thinks I will suddenly be born again and vote the right way on gay marriage?

While the potential of a nomination battle for my own seat had loomed since the moment I'd decided to voice my opinion on David Emerson's appointment, it was still only a wild theory that my own party might be behind the move. But still, the facts were disturbing.

In July, at the famous Troy's Diner meeting at which he had inflamed local Conservatives by telling them to strike a candidate search committee, Conservative organizer Wally Butts had ultimately retreated. "If you want Garth," he'd said, "then just wait until the next writ is dropped and do your quick nomination meeting then." They were words that put my supporters completely at ease, as they were apparently intended to do.

Two weeks later, on August 4, the party's national caucus met for a summer retreat in a bunker of a building in Cornwall, used to train air traffic controllers. Outside, hulking Great Lakes freighters drifted by on the broad St. Lawrence while two old Tudor jets kept watch from the top of their cement tethers. Inside there was trouble. In the midst of the Israeli-Hezbollah conflict many caucus members were eager to discuss the prime minister's bold and surprising Israel-at-all-costs position, especially when Israeli forces started to inflict heavy casualties upon Lebanese civilians.

Mr. Harper had been categorical in his defence of Israel, and was represented in Toronto on the night of July 26 by Parliamentary Secretary Colin Carrie at a major rally attended by eight thousand people. It raised $6 million for Israel in the first fifteen minutes and featured as the keynote speaker Charles McVety.

Carrie reported to Harper, as we sat in a session of Ontario caucus in Cornwall (the only one Harper had attended since the election), that the prime minister had been cheered as a hero that night. Harper responded by saying, "We will never let our friends in Israel down. Never."

But in the full national caucus that took place hours later, following a lengthy briefing on the situation by Peter MacKay and with Harper watching, an attempted debate on the issue was crushed. Led by Senator Anne Cools, who tried to question the pro-Israeli stance and ask why Canada was not taking a more balanced position, caucus members lined up at the microphones were told to take their seats. "There is no time for this," chair Rahim Jaffer yelled at Cools. "Sit."

Immediately Doug Finley took the stage and spent the last twenty minutes of the caucus talking about polling and, in his final Power-Point overhead, laid out the rules for MPs' nomination meetings. Nominations would begin immediately and be all over with by the time Parliament resumed on September 20, he said. Ridings would be "released" for nominations by the central party on a schedule of its own choosing. MPs would be informed in due course. The meeting was immediately adjourned, no questions.

Driving home that evening, forced off the 401 at Kingston by a transport rollover, I called Esther to tell her Finley's news and ask her to call Conservative Party headquarters and find out when Halton would be "released" for its nomination. She spoke with Joseph Dow, the young man Finley had appointed as director of political operations for Ontario, who refused to co-operate. Perplexed, I then called Dow myself, and he would only say that thirty of the 124 incumbent-held ridings had been released the previous day and he again refused to tell me when Halton would be opened up for any challenger to take me on.

This was strange behaviour for a political party remotely interested in protecting an incumbent-held riding. There was no reason why Ottawa could not let a riding get on with the process of establishing a period of time in which anyone could challenge an MP, if they could come up with a thousand bucks and two hundred names. But, in the dead of summer, during peak vacation time, and with no prospect of an election on the horizon, it would be tough for any MP to motivate hundreds of people to come out and fight a serious comer. Clearly, with the vague threats McVety had been making, in this context, I would be looking for all the advance warning possible.

That midnight, Finley sent me an email. "I don't want to call you this late at night but if you, your staff or campaign team have any issues, problems, or concerns with the nomination process," he wrote, "I'd be happy to discuss them with you. I'm generally available from 9 a.m. to midnight, seven days a week."

I called immediately, and got voice mail, as was repeated over the next four days. By August 9, we had not heard any news of the nomination release date, and were only ten days from the last possible time at which it could be called to meet the pre-Parliament deadline. I called once more. Finley answered.

"We originally were going to release you on the fourteenth," he said, "but we will let you go on Friday. And I'm telling you this in strict confidence, you understand." That was in two days. "They'll be doing a demon dialer to your members to inform them, and when that happens, the nomination period begins. But rest assured," he said in his Scottish brogue, "the rules have been set up to protect incumbents, but to make things look transparent. There are going to be one or two guys who are challenged, but that will be in the West. No worries."

On Friday night, August 11, at about 8 p.m., the recorded message was called through to members. There would be nine days for new memberships to be sold, and a nomination meeting—if any challengers emerged—would take place thirty days later, on September 11. But, Finley had said, no worries.

Trusting nobody, I wrote a letter of warning to all seven hundred members, asking for support if it were needed in a month, and mailed it that afternoon. On Saturday I headed for my half-renovated cottage on Lake Erie, thinking about the nomination process but also mindful of what Finley, Harper's chief political guy, had promised me. The riding release date had been a strict secret even from me, except for the two days' advance notice. The telephone message had not been sent out until Friday night, and it had only gone to existing members of the local Tory association—a list I had pored over, and was confident contained no challengers. And, "No worries"—a battle was not expected.

"Holy shit," Scott said Monday night when we spoke, after Esther had called with the news. "They just floored me with that call. They had my name and number as a riding member. They had organizers and an office somewhere. They had a telephone script, and they've got meetings already set up. How in the hell did they manage to set all of that up over the weekend? Since Friday night?"

But they didn't of course. It was the fourteenth, and they'd always been ready for the fourteenth, the day the party had set for Halton.

Scott called back a few minutes later. "Holy shit," he said again. "I just heard who the candidate will be: D'Arcy Keene."

On Tuesday morning, the fifteenth of August, 2006, just five months and twenty-one days after being elected an MP, there were a potential thirty days left in my political career. If the nomination were lost at this point in the electoral cycle, I'd be the lamest of ducks, effectively repudiated by my own community party members.

At 4 a.m. I went for a walk on the dark beach, mulling over what was known to me at that moment. Fact: the nomination would be contested. Fact: the forces lining up against me looked perfectly organized and fully deployed. Fact: an experienced adversary would be my opponent. Fact: the "righteous Right" was involved, capable of mobilizing untold numbers of instant Tories. Fact: this would be about refusal to condemn same-sex marriage. Fact: I'd understood from Finley I had the inside track on the nomination date. Fact: it was the worst possible time to mobilize support. Fact: Ian Brodie was a giant step closer to getting his way—what caucus would not be able to pull off, the "locals" might. Fact: I was, as George would say, nicely fucked.

Political nominations constitute the purest form of democracy, and also yield up its most dangerous moments. The candidate who emerges is the one who has the greatest number of supporters in a single hall on one night. George knew this well in 1988, when I hired him as a gunslinger to win the Conservative nomination in a huge new riding called Halton Peel. I was up against three seasoned candidates, one of whom was a national party director. The first political meeting I went to was an all-candidates debate, in which every single person in the room was wearing his badge.

My win came from attracting huge numbers of new people, and having enough free beer in the parking lot to keep them interested in staying through three ballots.

But this time would be different. No election coming. Political fatigue just months after the last vote. No popular understanding of what the hell this process was all about. Almost no time to organize or sign up new members. Vacation days. And, above all, a formidable opponent: God's army. The perfect political storm.

So, while my loyal supporters were about to start phoning and faxing, emailing, and selling, I figured the battle would be lost quickly if Keene was able to deliver up a couple of congregations. Our ground war could do only so much, therefore an air war had to begin. I went back down the beach, looking at the first shards of the sunrise, grabbed my laptop and by 7 a.m. had emailed a release to every major media outlet in the riding, the region, and the nation. There was just one shot at this.

Religious Right targets Garth Turner
Aims to defeat outspoken MP in riding nomination over gay marriage

Opponents of same-sex marriage are targeting outspoken Halton MP Garth Turner for defeat in a Conservative nomination battle set for next month. Members of religious groups held one organizational meeting in Milton this week and are seeking a candidate to oppose Turner and who would vote to open the divisive marriage issue.

"I can't say I am surprised by this," Turner says, "since I have been critical for months of those in the Righteous Right who I believe are intolerant and want to impose their moral code. I am quite convinced the majority of people in Halton do not want to debate gay marriage, but that doesn't mean this group—if it is well organized—can't scoop off the Conservative nomination.

"The rules certainly favour any group who can sign up instant members and then stack a meeting," Turner says. "And while that is democracy in action, and I respect it, this also means a special interest candidate can emerge whose views might be completely at odds with the majority of people who live in this riding.

"I am also concerned Halton might lose the independent voice I have tried to give it since becoming the MP. During the election campaign, people told me they wanted less party in politics and a much stronger voice telling Ottawa what families here want. It would be a shame to have a single-issue candidate who just doesn't care about having Town Hall meetings, or an online presence, or who will speak out on the tough issues when they arise."

Turner says he is 100 percent committed to fighting for the nomination in Halton, "because the last thing we need is an MP who cares only about people who think the way he does. That kind of politics is destructive."

I shut the laptop, woke Dorothy and the dog up, stumbled over boxes of floor tile and stacks of one-by-six pine that would remain uninstalled for months, and went back out on the beach for a last few breaths of summer air. I had campaigned my ass off for nine months and knocked on thousands of doors to become a member of Parliament. I'd done it this time for reasons of principle, not person. To be a faithful representative, not a party shill. To try and prove that an MP can be relevant, and not just another vote. And, I had to admit, things were not going too well. The prime minister. The party. The caucus. The backroom boys. And now God.

Who else could I piss off?

It took but a few hours for experienced, summer-weary national political reporters to strip the meat from the bones. By noon Canadian Press had picked up the story under the headline, "Conservative MP facing possible challenge from anti-gay marriage candidate." D'Arcy Keene made the predictable early mistake and, flattered to have a national news outlet on the phone, said far too much. And it could have been Ian Brodie in his throat.

"Our party's platform was pretty clear in the last election, that we're in favour of reopening the debate on the same-sex issue, and now Garth says he's not in favour of reopening the debate. Garth is a bit of a rogue agent, and since his election he's consistently gone after different groups and got them riled up against him … people of faith, of whom there are a fair number in this community, deserve to have their voices heard just as much as the next person."

Back in the riding I helped Esther, now on instant vacation from her duties in the riding office (since I was not allowing any MP's resources to be used in this skirmish), get our resources mobilized. By noon, amazingly enough, new party memberships started flowing

in as the news spread on television and radio (as I had planned) that
my political future was under serious attack. During the course of the
day I personally sold a couple of dozen ten-buck memberships and
was overwhelmed at the growing response. The publisher of one of
the community papers called to say he was bringing over memberships purchased by his entire staff. An environmental activist, who
five months ago considered me the walking equivalent of Suncor,
signed up his entire street, and suddenly we had more seniors walking in ready to work than we had letters to fold or envelopes to lick.

By two o'clock, though, the big news was McVety. Like Keene, he
could not pass by a microphone without preaching into it. The first to
tell me that the Toronto evangelist was freely admitting he was backing the campaign to unseat me was a *National Post* reporter. Now, of
course, there was a more worthy target that could be portrayed for
what he was—a man of the cloth who had instructed his flock that
homosexuals were "abominations" and was freely trying to manipulate
the democratic process to get single-issue candidates elected under
the banner of a party he thought he controlled, at least in part.

CP moved a second story, in which McVety said of me, "He has
this disease called entitlement . . . where, because he won a nomination meeting at one point in time, he's now entitled to it, and if anyone even dare talk about challenging him, they have breached his
entitlement.

"For two years, we have been encouraging grassroots Canadians
to get involved in the process, and especially work against anti-marriage
candidates."

It was working. The media material started to flow out in a steady
stream all day, as the reporter calls continued to come in. McVety now
could not shut up. He had been handed something even more valuable
than the ability to install his puppet candidate in a GTA riding that
D'Arcy Keene could never win: a media pulpit. A mainstream media
pulpit. A national, mainstream media pulpit.

"He feels he has the God-given right to be a member of Parliament," McVety told the *Toronto Star*. "If you challenge that, you're the devil incarnate."

"Mr. Turner has been viciously attacking us on his website for months now, and using his camaraderie with journalists to push his conspiracy theories," he told Dierdre McMurdy of the *Ottawa Citizen*. "He's got a sense of entitlement about his office, which is the very essence of the problem of corruption in politics."

"We're encouraging our mailing list in that region to get involved in the nomination process," McVety told the *National Post*, "and vote for D'Arcy Keene." Mr. McVety added that there were four hundred thousand names on his list.

Shit.

✧

Esther and I stared at each other over the hands-free and could scarcely believe what we were hearing from Joseph Dow. It was now less than twenty-four hours since "Shannon" had called Scott Nicholl on behalf of "the Conservative Party of Canada," and the calls were continuing. Every few minutes, one or the other of us was hearing from a local Tory association member who was being recruited for the Keene-McVety team, and in each instance the national party name was being used.

"Why is the Conservative Party doing this?" was the typical question. We had no answer, which led Esther to dial the number of the Political Operations for Ontario.

"This is completely wrong, it's false and misleading," Esther barked into the phone, "unless you're about to tell me that the party is actually behind this." It was also evident that the McVety forces were in possession of a current association membership list, something forbidden until a candidate had filed an application, been interviewed by a local committee, and then approved by national headquarters. Keene, as yet, had failed to even be in touch with the candidate nomination committee that the riding association had been instructed by Wally Butts to create.

The call deteriorated as the minutes passed. Apparently Dow had learned well that the party, not the candidates or their volunteers nor the grassroots members of the party, were actually in charge. It was an attitude consistent with one that he had shown as a young field organizer, then as part of the elections communications team in the war room with twenty-five-year-old Reform Party veteran Jenni Byrne. Brodie had recently raised eyebrows when he put Byrne in charge of hiring of departmental chiefs of staff, policy experts, and communications directors shortly after the January election, a function normally left to ministers, not the PMO. Byrne is the spouse of Ottawa-area MP Pierre Poilievre, later parliamentary secretary to Treasury Board president John Baird, and former staffer to Stockwell Day, now Stephen Harper's Security Minister.

Just six months prior to this call, in which we were looking to our own party for impartiality in a process imposed upon us by Ottawa, Dow and Byrne had acted as Doug Finley's eyes and ears in the ridings. It was their job to keep candidates under control, make sure the party's messaging was consistent, and that the leader was not embarrassed or surprised.

Dow would go on a few weeks later to make headlines as the key political operative accused of engineering the controversial by-election candidacy of Christian candidate and former city mayor Dianne Haskett in London North Centre. Ms. Haskett was living in Washington at the time, having worked for several years for a Republican senator. Dow gave local Tories just eight days' notice of a forced nomination meeting after previously informing Haskett of the date, and affording contenders little time to organize.

"He [Dow] was in charge and he was telling me what to do,"

Conservative riding association exec John Sterling told the *London Free Press*. "She [Haskett] was in the know about this nomination meeting prior to me knowing. She told me. Not only did she tell me she knew prior to me, I was told by Joseph Dow she knew before me. Joseph Dow was the guy in Ottawa I took my orders from."

At the time, Dow's actions were dismissed by Stephen Harper's director of communications, Sandra Buckler. "They're going to get a candidate, then we're going to have a run in the by-election whenever it's called. And hopefully we'll win." Ms. Haskett won the nomination and within one hour, Joseph Dow had issued a press release noting that her first election sign had been planted. During the campaign, which the prime minister called almost immediately for November 27, Ms. Haskett, a devout evangelical, was criticized for her past record of anti-gay statements. In 1997 she was fined $10,000 by the Ontario Human Rights Commission for, as mayor, disallowing a gay event.

On November 27, she finished third, behind Liberal Glen Pearson and the Green Party leader Elizabeth May, who increased her party's vote in the riding by 400 percent.

Esther asked Joseph Dow, point blank, if the party had tipped off McVety of the nomination date prior to the MP having been informed, and if D'Arcy Keene and the televangelist had been provided, contrary to party rules, with a membership list.

He refused to answer. But he did say he had "great respect for the ethics of Dr. McVety."

The sign taped onto the door of the Milton Sports Centre read, "Canadian Values meeting, Room 2." When I walked in, there were six of my supporters sitting around the big, squared table, trying to make like they didn't know each other. Another half-dozen people were there, three of whom introduced themselves as ministers or pastors. I sat, and two minutes later D'Arcy Keene walked in, looked at me, said the meeting had been hijacked, and stormed out.

In the hallway, Keene was talking earnestly on a cellphone. Pacing with him was a tall, thin man with snowy white hair that I was sure I'd seen somewhere before. I had. It was Rondo Thomas.

Thomas, as I have mentioned, is the second-in-command to Charles McVety at Canada Christian College, where he is also Dean of Bible Studies. In addition, Thomas is a pastor of the Toronto Christian Centre and fulfilled the same function in the Canadian military as well as being a missionary in the Arctic. A long-time Conservative, he and Charles McVety managed to achieve the nomination in Ajax-Pickering in 2005, taking on Liberal Mark Holland in the 2006 general election.

In an article published in the *Globe and Mail* in May 2005, McVety described the process used to snare the nomination for Mr. Thomas against former Mulroney-era Conservative MP René Soetens:

"The Defend Marriage Coalition engaged in a concerted effort to help pro-marriage candidates become nominated," Dr. McVety said.

"There is a desire to see pro-marriage nominees as candidates right across the country. We know that we have 141 pro-marriage MPS now, and our hope is to achieve a pro-marriage Parliament.

"The distortion of the separation of church and state has driven people of faith out of the leadership, and this is very wrong," he said. "And now that the government has decided to redefine marriage, faith leaders have been forced to urge their congregations to mobilize politically," McVety said.

"They are typically signing up members of political parties, some of them for the first time in their lives. Many of them are signing up for political parties they've never voted for before in their lives."

Mr. Thomas, who lost significantly to Mark Holland, came to media prominence during the campaign when videotaped giving a speech claiming Adam and Eve lived six thousand years ago and walked with the dinosaurs, a creationist belief voiced previously by Stockwell Day. "There is going to be a clash of morality views between those who believe in righteousness and those who believe in immorality, and when we collide there is going to be a conflict," Mr. Thomas says on the tape. "It doesn't matter what the media says, it doesn't matter what the government says. The facts don't count. We are going to win this conflict."

Mr. Thomas was also quoted as saying of same-sex marriage, "This would allow me to marry my sister, my mother, my daughter, or my grandmother. And when we try to change God's laws, the end result has to be total anarchy." Rondo Thomas missed several all-candidates debates during the 2006 campaign, and the Conservatives were accused of hiding him from reporters, with a special party handler assigned to keep the candidate from the media.

Mr. Thomas had apparently been asked by Dr. McVety to come to Halton and do for D'Arcy Keene what had been done for him in Ajax-Pickering when the nomination hall was stacked with instant members: "Many of them are signing up for political parties they've never voted for before in their lives."

That night, after a day in which scores of new members were signed up by my team, in which donations flooded in and in which emails, media calls, and blog comments were overwhelming, I posted the following:

> This is not a contest about who gets to sit in a green chair in the House of Commons. It's not about my job. This is about the kind of country you want. My opponents, led by Keene's benefactor, Charles McVety—Canada's Jerry Falwell clone—have stated clearly that I've been targeted. They are pouring resources into Halton to accomplish that. And my crime?

They say it's about my stated view that the same-sex marriage issue is better left behind us. They use code words like "people of faith" to draw a line between me and them. I'm on the wrong side. They decry my actions and statements which show I do not always walk in lockstep with the Conservative Party brass. Critics say I am too independent and not a team player. They quote my articles which state McVety's army is bigoted and intolerant and does not represent the majority of Canadian people. They call themselves pro-family instead of anti-gay. McVety clearly states that religion and politics should mix, and is able to point to many members of the Conservative caucus to prove his cause.

But this is actually about the imposition of a religious moral code on a secular country. It's about using a summer lull to scoop off a political prize which would be elusive when more people are paying attention. It's all about the tyranny of the well-financed minority versus the freedom of open democracy where all the people vote. Not a couple of buses of followers—but everyone.

So, this is not about the next election and who will be the Conservative candidate in Halton. If it isn't me, well, I'll get over it. But what I will not retreat from is the pursuit of a country where the doors and windows are opened up on the political process. Where people believe their leaders are representing them, not preaching to them. Where there is actually a role for consensus and cooperation. Where tolerance and hope are more important than any ideology. And where political parties and the people who lead them remember they are like trees: only as enduring as the roots that sustain them.

So, I'm pumped for battle. We all are. We are not going to waver in front of McVety's righteous talk. We will not look over our shoulders for party reinforcements. We stand firm. This may be called Halton, but it's really your town, your neighbourhood, and your Canada. It's worth the fight.

At 2:38 a.m., Doug Finley sent me an email. "You do love rheto-ric," he wrote. "Just call me. I'd prefer that this private email exchange was between you and I. It shouldn't be part of any blog. Not news-worthy anyway." I phoned. My call went to voice mail.

The next night McVety staged his second organizational meeting in Halton. It was better attended, and protected by a bouncer. Our plant inside reported a goal of five hundred new members within seventy-two hours before the nomination deadline was established, and Keene claimed to have personally signed "150 to 200" new Tories.

By Friday we had teams of canvassers going from door to door soliciting support. The local Federation of Agriculture had submitted a slew of new members. Members of the local Rotary club had adjusted their coming meeting so Rotarians could come to the nomination meeting. The campaign office was packed with volunteers, and we had arranged for one person to fly the new memberships to Ottawa on Sunday afternoon, in addition to submitting them online, so they could be hand-delivered to party headquarters. This had diverted 100 percent of my attention away from what I was supposed to be doing, which was being an MP. It also was pitting Conservative against Con-servative, secular against religious, and reopening the nomination fault lines that had been sealed over months before. McVety was now telling any reporter who would listen that this was a fight for reli-gious freedom and tolerance.

That afternoon I went to the New Life church in Milton, the largest congregation of fundamental evangelical Christians in the rid-ing. At that point I had no idea what forces McVety would be able to muster, or exactly how screwed I might be. The pastor, Dan Regge, had seemed like a reasonable and accessible guy when we'd met on two occasions, and I'd warmed to his long blond hair and cowboy boots.

I hoped he would have some insights into McVety's inroads into the faith community in the riding, and give me some advice. I was right on both counts. He told me, yes, McVety had been in touch and had lobbied hard, asking for help in unseating me. But Regge had not done so, saying I was not worthy of defeat. It was a defining moment.

At 2:36 a.m. Reverend Dan posted this on the blog:

Garth, I would like to publically apologize on behalf of all Evangelical Christians across Canada. Many of us disagree with SSM but we do not condone this militant, devious, looking for loopholes type of attack; this is not Christ-like behaviour. Please visit more Evangelical Churches in the area and you will see and feel the love of many true, genuine Christians.

Praying for you.

"I can assure you," Doug Finley was saying, "that the prime minister was not behind this. He made it clear to me, there was to be no 'get Garth Turner' thing. And so I've been working the phones quite hard for two days to kill this."

It was Friday night, five days after the McVety machine had rolled into Halton. Finley's unexpected call was extraordinary.

"I talked with McVety some time ago, and I asked him not to do it. I can tell you now, he's pissed off with you due to the interchange. He's so focused on you that he left Prentice and Moore and Keddy alone." He referred to then Indian Affairs Minister Jim Prentice, of Alberta, a suspected supporter of same-sex marriage, along with known progressives James Moore from BC, then parliamentary secretary to Michael Fortier, and Nova Scotia MP Gerald Keddy.

Finley was dismissive of McVety. "I'm telling you that I asked my guys to keep an eye on him, and they've been all over McVety, I've got spies everywhere—he's got no lift at all in your riding. He had big promises from the Knights of Columbus and others, but they failed to deliver the required numbers today.

"The top echelons of McVety's organization are very upset by this, but I said to them that this is absolutely ridiculous and they've got to find a way out. Jesus, they only sold thirty-seven memberships last night."

Then Finley told me that D'Arcy Keene, at 2:30 that afternoon, had instructed that a media release be prepared withdrawing his candidacy. It was over.

At the same time McVety was on the phone, giving an interview to Mike De Souza, of CanWest News, saying of me, "This is damaging against the Conservative cause, and we want him stopped."

Charles McVety, uncharacteristically, had lost the battle. Certainly not the war.

In the jihad between the religious Right and the blogging MP, the Internet turned out to be the battlefield. My initial conflict with the televangelist did not end with a regional television program, but spilled over to a digital audience of hundreds of thousands through my own blog and the zealous reaction to it. The evangelical community, and McVety in particular, are constantly online, their interrelated websites and specialty news services pumping out dedicated content. It took only hours for my "Taliban" comment to be spread across a broad network, used as an example of my so-called attack on Christian values—the values our "born-again" prime minister personified.

My defence, however, was also digital. The blog mobilized support, sold needed memberships, raised cash, and kept the media hooked on a Lilliputian battle for the right to represent a single riding. It gave me the credibility to raise the bar of interest until McVety found himself targeted by reporters who saw this for what it was—an assault on the democratic system by a TV preacher and media hound. In the end, however, it bought only time.

The blog had saved me from a quick and decisive death at the hand of Ian Brodie. It leapt from digital to mainstream print reality, garnered a huge instant audience, and kept me from being swept out of caucus just days after arriving. The blog had rescued me from my own colleagues anxious to cast me from the tent. It gave me the profile and following that weakened their resolve. And the blog had spared me from the persecution of the religious Right, who suddenly faced a barrage of difficult questions about motivation and process.

But, equally, being a digital MP was at the heart of my problems. It led to my ouster from the party I'd always been a part of. It put me in conflict with the leader of the country. In many eyes, it turned me into a maverick, renegade, and, worst of all, an untrustworthy colleague in a profession where only loyalty matters. It likely forever ruined my political career, at least so long as the country is ruled by cliques and special interests.

In so doing, however, it's helped carve a path forward. Blogging is crude and unreliable. So was giving everyone a vote.

CHAPTER FIVE

"Nobody asked you to have any ideas."

—Guy Lauzon, MP, Conservative National Caucus Chair, 2009

NINE MONTHS LESS TWO DAYS after being elected, Harper stood in national caucus and said, unexpectedly, that $1 billion in cuts to program spending had been identified by cabinet and would soon be announced. Then he turned his face up from his notes.

"There will be impacts in some of your ridings," he told the room. "They will affect people, and you may be tempted to talk about them. But don't. Anyone who has anything to say about this will soon find out they have a very short political career." I looked across a row of chairs, and saw several MPs exchanging disturbed glances.

Veteran Calgary member Lee Richardson was beside me. He listened, looked at me askance, and said under his breath, "Well, that's pretty fucking clear, wouldn't you say?" And it was. The government was about to chop unknown programs with unknown consequences to voters, and the MPs who represent them would not be told in advance, not have a chance to influence the decision, not be able to comment afterwards or defend the interests of their ridings.

Unless, of course, they wanted to become independents.

The tone for the Harper interlude in Canada's democratic history had been set early, back at our initial caucus meeting. Well-veined, wiry hands gripped both sides of the prime ministerial podium, with its velvety green covering, as Ray Speaker stared at the room. "My best advice to you," he started, and then paused a bit, as if to choose his words extremely well.

After all, each verb and sentence was important for the seventy-one-year-old veteran politician. This was likely his last political speech, the final time on a national stage. It had been forty-three years since he entered politics as a Social Credit radical in Alberta, and nine years since he'd left these Parliament buildings as a pillar of the Reform Party, its finance critic and House Leader. Now he was back, standing in the PM's place, speaking to the first federal government national caucus of his life, as a member of Prime Minister Stephen Harper's transition team. He was steadfast, but unsteady. Impressive, but spent.

"My best advice to those of you who will not be a part of the government," he said to a room of people, all awaiting a call from the prime minister or the whip, "is to be loyal to your party, do the work that you are asked, take your language training and perhaps in a couple of years, you might be asked to be a parliamentary secretary."

Four feet away, Stephen Harper led the applause, smiled, thanked the Reform pioneer, and resumed his seat. And while it may have been easy for the newbies in caucus to dismiss the words as political wallpaper, they were spoken deliberately—each sentence put together for a reason, and delivered as strategy. Harper's style of government, his management philosophy, and his use of people was being defined at that moment. Those who failed to listen would pay a price.

Stephen Harper, naturally, well knew his power. His grip here was unflinching. And how could it not be? Of 123 caucus members, at least eighty would get a call telling them they had a new title and, quite possibly, more money—up to $70,800 a session, in addition to basic pay of $155,000. In some cases it would mean a sizable personal support staff, global travel, national profile and media attention, departmental office and staff, car and driver, and palatial personal Hill office.

The favours about to be handed out would include cabinet posts, parliamentary secretary jobs, caucus chair positions, standing committee chairs, or working with the whip, House Leader, or PMO. In all, of the people sitting in the Reading Room that late January morning, two of every three would be getting at least new business cards, if not a compensation package that would boost their parliamentary pensions for the rest of their lives. The stakes could hardly be higher.

So, Ray Speaker's message had meaning. And the sense was clear: please the prime minister, and you will be pleased. It was the articulation of a reality now well embedded in federal political life, and constituted one of the greatest incentives a new member of Parliament might have to forget he or she was working for the people, and to start working for the PM, and the party. It was, as Mr. Speaker said, his "best advice."

As I sat there, making notes, I was struck by the emphasis this caucus was placing on the theme of unquestioning, blind discipline. Charlie Mayer and Pierre Vincent had made it clear the role of caucus members was to avoid the media at all costs and stick with the team in every regard, in every circumstance. Now Ray Speaker had spoken clearly as well—your ticket is ours to give. Behave, and be rewarded.

Some of the same things I'd heard in this room before, during almost six years of Conservative caucus meetings under Mulroney, then Kim Campbell. I would hear echoes of them again, from Stéphane Dion in the Liberal caucus across the hall. And while they, like every leader before and after, were in the business of buying loyalty with favours and high office, never had the message been so strident, so loud, or so crass. There was a new sheriff in town. A cowboy.

But I also sat there as an MP who'd just spent the better part of a year telling people exactly what they could expect from me. And this wasn't it. Already I sensed a conflict brewing between my sense of responsibility to the voters and the subjugation being demanded by the guys at the front of the room. It was clear no phone call would be

coming to my BlackBerry, and I had not expected one. But would I
even be able to survive? When compromise was asked for, when
inevitably the whip or the prime minister asked that the party be
placed before an MP's ultimate responsibility to the people who sent
him here, what would the answer be?

I already knew it. And with no sense of what was to come—Emerson, Lebanon, McVety, income trusts, the green plan, gun control,
same-sex marriage, the Quebecois nation—it was clear this would
probably end badly. The choice, then, was a simple one: decide to
compromise and get along, or put principle over party.

A mild, wet snowstorm was blanketing Ottawa the March night I
drove across the Island Parkway bridge, over the Ottawa River rapids,
into Aylmer. In a typically run-down Legion, through the bar and in
the back room, about a hundred members of the Aylmer-Hull Conservative riding association were gathered for their annual general
meeting.

This is one of the most Liberal ridings in Canada, represented by
a Grit in every election since it was created in 1914, but bravely contested in 2006 by Gilles Poirier, a lovable guy who takes Spanish lessons in his spare time and secured 17 percent of the vote for the Tories.
The riding association president was a campaign aficionado of my
blog, and this led to my invitation to address the bilingual crowd that
night. Once again, the thread binding me to the people was digital,
beyond the reach of a prime minister or party.

("I was warned about having you come to speak," he told me
moments before I did. "But I'm a bit of a rebel myself. And we need you.")

Meanwhile my newly minted Hill office was asked for a copy of
the speech by a couple of reporters, and bits of it ended up being
reprinted the following day. While I said nothing in this talk that had

not been spelled out a dozen times online, it didn't take long for the shit to hit the fan.

There is nothing more that I want. The prime minister has nothing I covet. I am completely challenged and fulfilled in trying to be the best MP in the world. And so, unlike many of my colleagues who want to be in cabinet or want to be parliamentary secretaries or want to have additional pay, more titles, a bigger office in a better building or a seat in the House of Commons closer to the boss, I don't care. And I don't think they should care, either. Because this MP thing is not about them.

We get elected because the people support us, and they make their decision based on many things. We come to Ottawa because they send us, not because we are called here by a greater force— party, or leader, or the cabinet table.

But too many MPs arrive and decide that being an MP, a representative of the people, is not good enough. They see the guys with the black cars and drivers waiting to carry them eight hundred feet to the next meeting. They see the opulent, unbelievable offices, the beautiful young staffers. They see the throng of microphones and cameras waiting for people who matter, while ordinary MPs slide by in obscurity.

And it does not take long—and I know this because I have experienced it in years past—before merely being an MP doesn't cut it anymore. Sometimes it takes only days. The first week. The first caucus meeting. Suddenly their personal goals become more important than the position they were given. Ambition wells up, stroked by leaders who know it is the narcotic that will turn an independent representative of the people into an employee looking for a fix. Title. Office. Power.

This is not what the people want, or voted for. They lose their voice when their MP is keeping quiet, being a team player, obeying the whip and looking to get ahead. And so is it really any wonder why, when the trust rankings came out last week, politicians finished dead last?

I am here to change that.

They gave me a standing ovation. It would be the last group of Conservatives I ever addressed.

The next morning the *Globe and Mail* carried a splashy column by analyst John Ibbitson with the headline, "Why Garth Turner is the future of politics." The recognition was great. The timing could not have been worse. Calling me "a digital populist," Ibbitson ended his piece prophetically: "Kick Garth Turner out of caucus? They'd be kicking out the future of Canadian politics."

Stephen Harper chose this day to have an unusual rally of MPS and staff, carefully staged for the national media, in Room 200 of the West Block. With a normal capacity of three hundred people, standing, the PMO had the place packed with eight hundred bodies. The set-up was elaborate and echoed the campaign—formal stage, TelePrompter, Rolling Stones-quality sound system, rear riser for TV cameras and pool media feed.

The prime minister performed well, and this was indeed the first opportunity for the majority of new Hill staffers to actually see the guy. He said nothing new, but said it with conviction. Speech over, RCMP and Hill security blocked all exits but one, and it took more than half an hour for people to squeeze and shimmy their way through the one remaining doorway. I occupied myself catching up on email on my Berry as I shuffled along, more or less oblivious to those around me.

"So what bullshit about the prime minister are you blogging now?" Looking up, I saw the towering, young, portly face of James

Moore, whom I had not met and vaguely recognized as an MP. His tone was combative and his look decidedly hostile. He was staring down at my Berry, and speaking loudly enough that everyone within a six-foot radius turned around to look at the person who was probably at that very moment plotting to bring down the leader they'd just crowded to hear.

Moore, who would not be thirty years old until the summer, had been an MP for six years, having come to Ottawa as an advisor to Preston Manning, cutting short a budding student radio career in BC. Voted "best up-and-coming MP" four years in a row, Moore made his mark as a Reform Party attack dog in Question Period. He was front and centre in 2005 when Belinda Stronach switched to the Liberals, saying in a statement bitterly delivered into a CTV camera, "I think it shows there are two kinds of people in public life—people with principle and people like Belinda Stronach."

A fierce Harper loyalist, Moore was apparently convinced he would be appointed to cabinet after the January 2006 win. On February 5, he wrote in his online blog, "A few words are seared into my brain that I've been saying for about two weeks now: Mr. Harper will announce his cabinet on Monday. I have nothing more to say." A month after being made parliamentary secretary to unelected cabinet minister Senator Michael Fortier, Moore was still smarting. "Anybody who doesn't get into cabinet is disappointed," he told the *Globe and Mail*.

Moore would be disappointed once again in the cabinet shuffle of January 2007, which saw Mr. Harper's inner circle swell with the addition of five new ministers, but without his face among them. Asked if he was disappointed, he told the local paper, "Sure, but it's hardly the end of the world. I am thirty years old. This is not my last grasp at an opportunity to serve in political office." When he said that, the man was a member of Parliament and a parliamentary secretary. But, obviously, it was not enough. Not until the summer of 2008 when, as a reward for defending Harper in the Chuck Cadman affair, he was made a junior minister, responsible for the 2010 Olympics and official languages.

Mr. Moore decided after the January election and the week after his first cabinet shutout to discontinue his own blog, breaking an election promise. "This blog is going to be a casualty of my new responsibilities and my prioritizing of my spare time," he wrote in his final entry. And James Moore made headlines again during the December 2006 Liberal leadership convention in Montreal, when he took partial credit for the elimination of candidate Bob Rae. As CTV reported, seconds after Mr. Rae withdrew from the race, which Stéphane Dion would win, Moore wandered the convention floor pulling out a handful of buttons mocking Rae. "There's a reason we handed out so many of these," Mr. Moore said. "Liberals don't know how to play poker . . . the NDP is also feeling happy right now." The buttons had slogans like "Make Bob the first NDP prime minister" and "Vote Bob. Who needs Ontario?"

At that convention some overly enthusiastic Conservatives were also reported to have created a bogus memo, signed by Doug Finley, which was leaked to newspapers and purported to show that Tories were most afraid of facing Michael Ignatieff and most anxious to have Bob Rae win.

I heard his voice again, as James Moore increased the volume and the attention I was receiving. "And would you happen to be webcasting from your glasses right now?" he thundered. Fortunately, the doorway approached. Moore receded, as I gave him my best, silent, piss-off look.

Mr. Ibbitson, evidently, had made an impact. There may have been eight hundred people in that room, but not room enough for one digital populist.

My words now chased me to the first meeting of Ontario caucus—the group which, seven months later, would be the willing and able instrument of my exodus from the party of Mr. Harper. My Hull speech of the night before and Ibbitson's column were both contained in the Library of Parliament daily clipping service, Quorum, which I noticed sitting in front of several caucus members when I entered.

Almost fifty people sat around the table when chair Gord Brown asked for each to make a few comments. One of the first to speak was John Baird, the newly minted president of the Treasury Board. He was in his shirtsleeves with a copy of the *Globe* in front of him and his Berry on top. At his right shoulder sat Diane Finley—Doug Finley's wife—the new minister of human resources, who had just been diagnosed with Graves' Disease, a condition that would lead her to wear sunglasses at all times. Baird was positioned almost opposite me. On my right was Senator Hugh Segal, and on my left rookie MP Mike Wallace, from the neighbouring riding of Burlington. Finance Minister Jim Flaherty was five places to Segal's right.

The room, at an instant, went tense.

"Mr. Chairman, we have to talk about Garth Turner," Baird said. "The media may love him, but he's hurting this party and this government by opening his mouth." It was the first four minutes of the first caucus, and Baird's attack was unexpected. "Who does he think he is? Who is Garth Turner to tell us what we should be doing here?"

Baird grabbed his BlackBerry and thumbed open an email. He read, holding the device out at most of an arm's length, ". . . but too many MPs arrive and decide that being an MP, a representative of the people, is not good enough. They see the guys with the black cars and drivers waiting to carry them eight hundred feet to the next meeting. They see the opulent, unbelievable offices . . ."

He looked at me for the first time, and asked, "Are you writing about me?"

John Baird is a professional politician and shares a warm relationship in official Ottawa with both Stephen Harper and his wife,
Laureen. Just a few months before this meeting, the leader of the
official opposition, as Harper then was, chose to kick off his national
election campaign in the Ottawa-West Nepean office of the new candidate there, thirty-six-year-old John Baird. Laureen then canvassed
with him, door-to-door.

Following the election, Laureen Harper was seen much more in
his company, asking him to escort her to social events when Harper
was out of town on business. In early October 2006, the two of them
made a stunning entrance on the red carpet at the fundraising gala
for the tenth anniversary of the National Arts Centre on the canal in
downtown Ottawa. Mr. Baird was reported as dashing in his tuxedo
while Mrs. Harper appeared in a gorgeous Sunny Choi gown and ear-
rings that she had designed to match the chandelier above.

When he was barely into his twenties, Baird went to work on Parliament Hill, on the political staff of Tory minister Perrin Beatty, staying on until the defeat of the Progressive Conservatives in 1993. He
then briefly became a lobbyist to the federal government before
winning a seat at Queen's Park, representing the riding of Nepean.
Mr. Baird quickly became immersed in the right-wing ideology of the
Mike Harris government, and joined cabinet in 1999 as minister of
community and social services, where he implemented the hugely
controversial workfare program that removed thousands of low-
income people from social assistance.

In 2002, Baird was the first cabinet minister to jump onboard Jim
Flaherty's leadership campaign. Each man had been elected in 1995,
and each had become hard-core Harris supporters, sharing an obvious bond. Flaherty made headlines with a proposal to jail homeless
people who refused assistance, and lost the campaign spectacularly to
Ernie Eves. Baird continued on as government whip, then energy minister, until the Conservative government was defeated in 2003.

Baird then co-chaired Flaherty's second attempt at leadership in two years, which Mr. Flaherty lost to John Tory. At the same time, Baird was supporting Stephen Harper in his bid to become leader of the new Conservative Party. He then co-chaired the federal party's Ontario campaign in the same year. Both Baird and Flaherty then left provincial politics in 2005 to campaign for the House of Commons.

In Parliament, John Baird quickly became the loudest and most combative member of the Harper government in daily Question Period, setting what many called a new standard for partisanship in an unruly House. In the November 2006 municipal election campaign, Mr. Baird was accused of unprecedented meddling when he held up a long-promised federal grant for a new Ottawa city light rail project that he opposed until a new mayor—an avowed Conservative—was elected, and killed the project.

Ontario caucus was not going exactly as I had contemplated it, and we were not even yet at the main event. John Baird was clearly indignant. He threw his Berry down on the table with a crack. The gesture had drama, and import.

My words on the nature of representation, the role of an MP, and the distorting influence of ambition on politics were not going down well in a caucus clearly uninterested in theory. Over the next months I'd understand better just how important the exercise of power was to the Harper team members, and would be struck at how many times the prime minister spoke in caucus about the majority government to come. Where I viewed becoming an MP as a goal achieved, and did not covet cabinet, merely being prime minister was clearly not enough for Mr. Harper, as merely being an MP would not have satisfied John Baird.

But, as noted, troubles this day—despite the *Globe*, the speech the night before, despite webcasting glasses and shattering the Harper ban on speaking to the media—were starting. The boundaries of an MP's world were about to be defined by a curiously pissed-off minister of finance.

Two promises Halton voters had heard consistently during the winter campaign was that tax reduction for middle-class families would be on my hit list, if elected, and that they'd be intimately involved in letting the new government know how the system could be improved. So, in the first post-cabinet caucus, I'd approached Jim Flaherty and asked if he would consider a report from my constituents on potential budget actions. He looked at me over his usual coffee cup, no saucer, and said, "Sure. Welcome it."

During February and March, this became a passion. A series of six Town Hall meetings were held across the riding, some of them exceptionally productive, packed, and emotional in the way people responded to the simple act of being asked. The net was widened, and people on the blog were asked to submit their ideas, as well as readers of my weekly column, carried in more than thirty newspapers across the country (a holdover from my pre-politician days). This was supplemented by a host of radio and television interviews, and suddenly, I had heard from more than seven thousand Canadians. There was a stack of printed emails two feet high in my home office, and the volume and quality of comments from coast-to-coast was arresting.

It was as if taxpayers were responding to a new dawn in the political system—a feeling that after thirteen years of top-down paternalistic government, finally, the doors and windows of Parliament were thrown open. It was thrilling to click onto every new message, open every new posting, read every new letter.

The blog was turning me into a digital MP for thousands of people across the country who, for the first time, felt they had instant access to the floor of the House of Commons, to a member, to a finance minister, to their government. They poured their lives over me. I was obsessed, hooked, addicted, high on the narcotic of populism and utterly convinced of the power of this experiment. Could it be that the people finally got to write policy to create a purer form of digital democracy? Why struggle with the rusty machinery of representative government, when governing could come from the bottom up, delivered in real time, in real words?

I worked night and day compiling the material, writing my report, revelling in change.

Jim Flaherty agreed to see me at a breakfast meeting in Toronto. I described to him what was happening, gave him some of the feedback I was getting, and told him of the immense goodwill that seemed to be swirling around his new job. They want you to be bold, I told him. Income-splitting, a family tax return, help with retirement savings, a flat tax. It's a time when people are looking to you and saying, why not?

He seemed pleased, flattered. I left the hotel, brushed off the inch of snow that had dumped on my car while we'd sat and watched tourists in their bathing suits splash through the indoor pool, and was truly encouraged. The next few days were immersed again in tabulations, text, interviewing independent taxation experts and economists from across the country. By mid-March, a dozen solid ideas had emerged, and been explained, supported, and contextualized in twenty thousand words.

On the blog, I reported to those who had been feeding in their ideas:

So, tonight my report is not yet done ... but the road map is there, the analysis is complete, the consensus opinion has emerged, and I have arrived at twelve recommendations. They range from the obvious tax policy changes I believe middle-class Canadian families want, to my conclusion that at least one major plank of the Conservative election platform should not be implemented, to a suite of broad and hopefully far-sighted initiatives that I believe only this government, and at only this time, can take.

Now, I have already run into some lowlifes who have asked me what happens if Flaherty ignores me, my contributors, and our collective recommendations. What if the geniuses in the Finance Department already have this figured out, and just give it to the new minister to read? What if none of our suggestions are listened to—will this exercise have been a failure?

And I say, absolutely not. Seven or eight or nine thousand people had some direct input into this report, and they probably talked it over with ten or twenty or thirty thousand other people. Then there are all the others who thought about the budget after reading one of my articles, or posts, or a newspaper account of one of my meetings. In all, this little project could have made tens of thousands of Canadians think a little harder about how they are taxed, how their government spends their money and what kind of country we are trying to build.

So, how can that be a failure? And is this not the kind of thing an MP should be doing, influential or not? Sure, anybody can be ignored, but since when should that stop us from speaking? If ideas are powerful enough, then they will find a way to bubble through whatever obstacles may be laid in their path.

On March 15, Flaherty called me and I filled him in more on the report's contents and recommendations. I also asked him if he'd agree to a photo op when I presented the thing to him, just so all the folks whose words were in there, including oodles of people from Halton, would know a promise had been kept. Absolutely, he said.

A few days later I went to see him in Ottawa, at the Department of Finance. Walking in to the ugly white office tower I could tell virtually nothing had changed since the last time I was here when Mike Wilson summoned me—except the security. In a post-9/11 world now, getting into any ministerial office is a chore.

Flaherty was friendly, accommodating, and gave me every last second of his time before having to jump into the limo and get to the train station for the 6 p.m. to Whitby. I took with me a copy of the finished report—all done, save for the printed covers and the cerlox binding that Carol and the others at the Milton print shop would add that weekend. I briefed him on the recommendations, as he took a few notes, and told him I'd be recommending against one of the campaign promises Stephen Harper had made. He took off those unique glasses of his—the half-lens reading glasses that fold away into a matchbook-sized case—and looked at me with some concern. The provision for rolling over capital gains tax should not go at this time, I told him. It is hugely expensive, will benefit relatively few, wealthy, people, and be a nightmare to administer.

He looked at me and said nothing. Flaherty smiled, took the report, put it in the open briefcase by his side, and said he had to make the train. "I will read this," he promised, "and get back to you some more."

The next day I emailed Rahim Jaffer, the chair of the national Conservative caucus, and asked for five minutes during the coming session to brief my colleagues on the contents of the report. I would be denied.

On March 23, in imminent anticipation of the release of the report, and secure in the knowledge the minister of finance had been not only utterly involved, but fully briefed, I issued a short media release to try to ensure my seven thousand budget-writing bloggers and constituents would get the attention they deserved. What happened next was also unexpected.

Tory MP urges party platform change
By STEVEN CHASE
(The *Globe and Mail*)

OTTAWA—Maverick Conservative MP Garth Turner is once again playing the thorn in his government's side, publicly calling on Prime Minister Stephen Harper to scrap part of the Tory election platform that he says is proving unpopular. But, while he issued a press release yesterday announcing this, the Ontario MP refused to identify which election plank he thinks his government should drop.

Mr. Turner said he's delaying releasing his recommendations until March 29, after he has delivered a copy to Finance Minister Jim Flaherty. "He may have to stand up and answer a few questions after I present him [with] the report, so I'd like him to see it first," he said.

He said he owes it to his party to give them a heads-up. "I have been enough of a surprise to my prime minister so far," Mr. Turner said.... "I don't think it's affordable, I don't think it's workable and I don't think it really jibes with our themes of doing the greatest good for the greatest number of people," he said of the plank he wants dropped....

The MP declined to confirm he wants the capital gains pledge shelved, but economists and tax experts have warned this promise needs to be significantly reworked and narrowed in scope or end up costing $1 billion to $2 billion annually instead of the $150-million estimated in the Tory platform.

The Prime Minister's Office responded quickly to Mr. Turner's press release, saying it had no intention of backing away from election promises. "We're going to fulfill our commitments," Mr. Harper's communications director, Sandra Buckler, said.

Almost instantly the blog was overrun with negative comments, which kept up for days. Typical was this:

Garth: Canadians voted for Mr. Harper's platform and you ran on it under the Conservative banner. Do you really think now is the time to break promises because you think you personally came up with a better idea? There are 125 people in your caucus, an entire department of experts working with our new Finance Minister who have insights you do not have nor do the 10,000 people you took feedback from. You are beginning to sound a lot like the Opposition finance critic instead of a member of government.

Jim Flaherty did not call me back, as promised. In fact, he never called me again.

Then, the night before the first Ontario caucus meeting, and two days before I was scheduled to release my report to the finance minister and Canadians for discussion, he made it clear in a BC speech that the capital gains tax plank in the election platform would be, for now, scrapped. "With respect to this particular initiative," Flaherty told the Surrey Chamber of Commerce, "we will be taking some time to consult Canadians before moving forward."

Just three days after Sandra Buckler had said, categorically, "We're going to fulfill our commitments," Mr. Flaherty had signalled otherwise. The minister of finance and his officials had also obviously reached the same conclusion I had—the capital gains promise Mr. Harper had hastily made in the final days of the campaign was far too complicated, narrow, and costly to be announced in the first Conservative budget. It was not going to happen.

That did not surprise. But Flaherty shocked.

Back to the next morning's Ontario caucus meeting. After John Baird's comments, Gord Brown encouraged people around the table to speak, and so they did, with Garth Turner and his soon-to-be-released budget report being the topic of choice. The reaction was devastating, even after I stood and outlined the major recommendations. Not that anyone cared, since it was process, not content, that was the issue.

"Nobody asked you to do this," Guy Lauzon said. "Nobody asked Garth Turner to have any ideas, or to run around and ask people what they think. We had an election, and we have a platform, and that's what we think. You are undermining every one of us. You have no right. No right."

Colleagues accused me of sideswiping them, and worse, of blindsiding the minister of finance. "I am so disappointed in you," Bev Oda said, "that you would do this to one of your colleagues, putting pressure on him from within, making him look bad, and, frankly, making us all look bad just so you can look good."

Watching Bev, I remembered sitting in her office in the CTV facility in what used to be Agincourt, on the 401 in Toronto's east end. I was the network business editor and on-air guy, and she was in programming. She was grilling me about what kind of mortgage to get—short or long—for the condo she was purchasing.

Finally the baton was passed to Jim Flaherty, and I relaxed a little inside. After all, I'd asked his permission to embark on this project, briefed him twice in person and once on the phone and given him an advance copy of the entire report in plenty of time to make changes. I'd explained to the finance minister why I wanted to do this, why I thought it was good politics to include so many people in its preparation and how an effective communications plan could be put together when it was presented. Let's show the people, I'd said, that the Harper team is ready to adopt a whole new approach in finally listening to the people on an issue as central as taxation. After all, it's their money.

The day before, my office had liaised with his, setting up a time and a place for the photo op when I'd put the report into his hand—at ten o'clock, on the way in to national caucus, outside Room 253-D of the Centre Block. We'd written a suggested media release, and sent it over for approval. We'd also prepared and printed the report in both languages, and had a summary of recommendations and sampling of taxpayer opinions printed and translated. Both French and English versions were ready to be posted online.

It would be okay. He knew. I took a breath, calmed, and waited for Flaherty—the number two guy in the government, the senior political minister for Ontario, and the most respected member of government in the room—to tell them to chill.

It's okay, he'd say. Garth and I talked about this thing from the start. He'd told me what he was doing and why, then he briefed me while he was writing it, and gave me a copy to go over. Actually, I agreed with him on that capital gains thing, as you know, and I thought he played a role in helping to dampen down people's expectations on it. So, no, hell, it's a good example of what an individual MP can do—to show we care what people think, and, you know, help a minister with positioning.

And I would be saved.

But Flaherty was having none of it.

He failed to acknowledge I'd ever spoken to him, or that he had been given an advance copy, or that I'd shared with him my findings on the capital gains platform plank. Instead he said what I had done "was not helpful." He denied having said in Surrey that the capital gains was shelved, and then, "This government will not be commenting on this report.

"Frankly, I don't know why he did it."

Gord Brown asked me not to release the report to the media the next day—the same time I'd planned to give it to caucus. Against my better judgment, but knowing Flaherty had just screwed me with finality, there was no option. Instead of going to reporters, it went to every Conservative MP's office, with a note asking for comments. Of 124 caucus members, only two did respond. Baird, Flaherty, and Oda were not among them.

My caucus colleagues, I wrote on the blog that night, *have watched me through one end of a media telescope, and often intensely disliked what they saw. My actions have been decisively independent, even brazen. While*

they expected me to be satisfied and reliable in lining up behind the Con-
servative agenda, I have been running around the country asking people
what they think. I have taken up causes nobody asked me to, and for goals
which may run counter to what my own party wants to accomplish....

To the best of my limited capacity, I understand this. I did not mean
to alienate some of these people. They did not ask it. Do not deserve it. And
I well realize that my voters, my constituents, and all Canadians will be
better, more quickly served, if I can find a way of working with the tide that
ebbs and flows across this strange Hill.

But, thus far, the lessons of caucus were clear. Be disciplined. Put
the team before the voters. Avoid media. Leave policy to others. Stop
blogging.

The Flaherty report was a profound disappointment. In fact, it was a
personal disaster. The national caucus had flatly refused an opportunity for raising the ideas for debate. The regional caucus attacked the
act of doing a report, without even caring about what was in it. I was
left without support or defence. The communications plan was left in
shambles, and when it was over, I looked like anything but a team
player. Worse, knowing the story above could never be relayed back to
the thousands of people who felt they were finally closer to government by responding to a single MP, I had to fold. I felt ill doing it.

On Wednesday morning there was no photo op with Minister Flaherty, no media release, and no budget reports handed out. Instead, at
the beginning of national caucus I just handed a finished report to Mr.
Flaherty and one to the prime minister. "Many Canadians, and my
constituents," I said, "would like you to have this." They both said
thank you, and that was it. Harper smirked.

Here is how I explained it. I wrote this on the blog that day, the
only way I could find to soften the issue. I am not proud of it. "But, I

am pleased to tell you, things worked out a lot better than I had expected. MPs made a point of asking for copies. Others seemed genuinely appreciative I acted to include them in the process. The media guys decided not to eat me up and spit me out for withholding the goodies from them. And caucus, which was long and intense, was actually also useful and productive. At the end of it—despite my obvious and public rift with the party gods—I am heartened."

What really happened: a caucus member from Alberta went to the mic after Harper had spoken and said, "Prime minister, I want you to be aware of a problem we have with Garth Turner. He thinks he can tell us what should be in the budget." Harper looked down at the report he had just been given. Then Larry Miller, a beef farmer MP from Ontario, got up and said, "Prime minister, we have already dealt with that in Ontario caucus."

A bullet dodged, and then another small act of kindness. A francophone MP whispered to me, standing near the door to the anteroom where the whip confiscated BlackBerries before each meeting. "I heard you talk about your budget ideas on CBC Radio," he said, "and I think they are *très bon*."

The next day the same member slid into the seat beside me in the House. He looked worried beyond words. "Has anyone asked you about me speaking to you in caucus?" he asked. "I think they saw me do that, you know, from the front. I hope not—I really need this position." I knew he was up for a parliamentary job with the Speaker's office. I also noticed his cuticles, pulled to the quick and bleeding.

It was just hours before budget day and Liberal finance critic John McCallum was stuffed onto one of the little square stools tucked into the back corner of the House of Commons foyer, while I was stuffed into the one beside him. Facing us was Mike Duffy, the reigning media god in the nation's capital. No stranger to adversity, Duffy had endured not only the ravages of a bad heart (with his biggest test still to come, in the autumn of 2006) but had also felt the sting of professional reversal.

I remembered well when I was at CTV in Toronto, and Duffy would fly in from Ottawa every Friday to command vast amounts of studio time and respect for his *Sunday Edition* show. Suddenly one day, it was capriciously cancelled by network management, convinced the world wanted more *eTalk Daily* than news that actually mattered. Duffy was banished to the low-budget cable operation NewsNet from where, now a few years later, he had emerged as both a sage and a star, against all odds.

And McCallum also had a history with me. When he was the dour chief economist at the Royal Bank, I used to take my camera crew up to interview him on Bank of Canada policy or leading indicators. John worked in a corner office on a top floor of the South Tower of the Royal Bank Plaza, looking across the lake through windows tinted with real gold. A career academic before he was a banker, McCallum never struck me as a man who would fancy politics until he asked for some advice one day. Just don't let them use you up, I said.

Mr. McCallum, of course, got elected and did well. Secretary of state for finance, minister of defence, minister of veterans affairs, minister of revenue. But today he was reduced to the role of an opposition politician scoring points, this time as the Liberal finance critic who was letting everyone know Jim Flaherty was about to destroy everything.

"It's a Robin Hood budget," he told Duffy. "Jim Flaherty is about to steal from the poor and give to his rich friends." McCallum laid down as proof the Tories' obvious intent to roll back the last Liberal income tax reduction, at the same time cutting a point off the GST, "so Porsches will cost less."

I lost that debate. McCallum was loud and dogmatic. The one-time recalcitrant bank economist had learned the lessons of Ottawa well—continue to talk when asked not to, talk over your opponent, make your point, repeat it then repeat it again, concede nothing, and smile confidently when done.

Actually, Budget 2006—delivered in the House of Commons by Mr. Flaherty at 4 p.m. on May 2, 2006—brought one or two more lessons on what the Stephen Harper Conservatives expected of their MPs. That pretty much amounted to sitting in your seat and clapping.

When the budget date was announced my office asked Flaherty's shop if I could attend the pre-budget lockup on Parliament Hill, gaining—like the journalists there—a few hours in advance to read the documents and prepare an independent analysis. This is exactly what I'd done countless times as a media guy, and as an MP for each of Mike Wilson's budgets the last time in Parliament. In the lockup I had produced a caucus communications newsletter called, cheekily, "This is NOT The Toronto Star," which was immediately faxed to every Tory riding association in the country (this was pre-email), then laid on the desk of each Conservative MP, while they were still sitting listening to Wilson deliver the goods.

A week before the budget, the Finance Department announced details of the media lockup, which would take place in the Confederation Ballroom of the Westin Hotel, two blocks off the Hill. Journalists would be let in at 10:30 a.m., after an hour-long security sweep of the room, and not let out again until Flaherty stood at four o'clock.

Two days later, Flaherty's chief of staff, David McLaughlin, announced a second lockup, this one for MPs' staff, to take place in a committee room in the West Block starting mid-afternoon. "We invite you to nominate one representative from your office to attend," his memo said.

The same day, the Department of Finance announced budget lockups for opposition MPs, including finance critics, leaders, deputy leaders, and other caucus officials. And yet another lockup was arranged for special interest groups, with Finance sending out between 150 and 200 invitations to bodies, of which eighty were expected to send spokespeople.

Many emails and voice messages later, the finance minister's press secretary, Eric Richer, had failed to respond to my request. Then, three days prior to the event, I was formally denied entry into any of the lockups. I sent this message to Jim Flaherty's BlackBerry: "Hi Jim. I wish to be in the budget lockup on Tuesday so (1) I can send an email blast to about 12,000 people on my distribution list, (2) I can complete some caucus-friendly constituency materials to give to my colleagues as you speak, and (3) I can finalize plans for a media event in my riding and in Ottawa the next day on the impact of the GST cut on new housing—I have arranged to do this with one of the biggest homebuilders in Canada. But your office tells me I absolutely cannot be in the lockup. This is not helpful, and certainly not consistent with my past experiences on the Hill. Can you help?"

No response. Then, a few hours before I would debate John McCallum on the eve of the budget, chief government whip Jay Hill sent this memo to all offices:

> Please note that MPs will not be allowed to attend the budget lockup tomorrow. However you have received a memo earlier outlining that you could nominate one representative from your office to attend. Also please note that all MPs are expected to be in the House when the budget is presented at 4 pm tomorrow.

Curious, I called the whip's office and asked Jay Hill why such a memo would be sent. "I have no idea," Hill said. "We're just doing what Flaherty's office instructed." Asked how many MPs had requested to be in the lockup, he answered, "Just you."

While this was not a major deal, the fact remained that the Harper government's first budget, eagerly awaited and symptomatic of what voters could expect in the future, would be reviewed in advance by journalists, opposition MPs, special interest groups, and Parliament Hill staffers, and yet Conservative MPs themselves were now banned. Not discouraged, but banned.

The reason why came with a phone call from Jim Flaherty's chief of staff, David McLaughlin. "We don't want freelancing," he said. "We will have caucus materials ready—talking points, stuff for house-holders. You'll have it in a few hours, and you will stick with the message. The minister wants this day to be about him, not about you."

On budget day, apparently understanding it would be not be helpful for Canadians to know that Conservative MPs, sent to Ottawa to form a government, were the only ones on Parliament Hill banned from knowing the budget's contents in advance, McLaughlin relented. I was allowed into the lockup that contained staff members from MPs' offices, and given ninety minutes to read the budget document. During that time a House of Commons security constable was posted near me.

I could only imagine what my constituents would think, had they been able to see me in the room in the Parliament buildings to which they sent me, under guard.

Jim Flaherty first shook my hand during the late summer of 2004 after climbing the stairs to my company's second-floor television studio on Bay Street, in the heart of the financial district. He was a month away from losing the provincial PC leadership contest on the second ballot to John Tory, a man Flaherty was describing, as he stood there waiting for the cameras to roll, as a Liberal in drag.

Tory, he said, was an urban, pro-abortion, pro-homosexual, big-government, unelected politician who basically could not be trusted with running Ontario. Flaherty, on the other hand, was the pro-marriage candidate, being supported once again by televangelist Charles McVety, of Canada Christian College.

A few weeks later, Flaherty would impress a lot of delegates with his convention speech—casual, off-the-cuff, in front of the podium, forcefully relaxed, and very focused. But it would not be enough, as the former Ontario finance minister lost 54 percent to 46 percent. There were apparently more metrosexuals in the provincial Progressive Conservative party than there were avowed social conservatives like Mr. Flaherty. Within a year, he would find a new political home with Stephen Harper's federal Conservatives, and finally win that seat in Parliament to become the second most powerful man in the land.

Jim Flaherty is, by anyone's standards, an achiever. He skated and stickhandled his way to a hockey scholarship at Princeton, then took a law degree at Toronto's Osgoode Hall, before setting up practice with Christine Elliott, whom he would marry. She went on to follow his political lead, running in Flaherty's old provincial riding and becoming a Conservative MPP.

Once at Queen's Park in 1995, he became a symbol of the right-wing "common sense revolution" of then-Premier Mike Harris, allying himself with social conservatives in caucus and then becoming labour minister in 1997, and attorney general two years later. Mr. Flaherty waged war on Toronto's "squeegee kids," the ragtag, wild-looking youths who every morning harassed and panhandled drivers from Mississauga and Whitby as they inched down off ramps from the Gardiner Expressway. Jim Flaherty also promoted an agenda item Christian groups had long demanded—tax credits for parents who send their kids to private or denominational schools. Many evangelicals are committed to seeing an end to the state-run educational system, which they view as too secular, and a return to religious-based education.

When Mike Harris quit in 2002, Mr. Flaherty launched his first leadership bid, running on a program of law and order, tax cuts, and selling off the provincial television network, TVO, as well as the hugely profitable Ontario-run liquor stores. He proposed banning strikes by teachers and criminalizing the homeless by jailing those who refused to sleep in shelters. He was the only candidate to declare himself pro-life, and pledged to allow no new abortion clinics if he became premier. As a result, Charles McVety announced his strong support of the Flaherty candidacy, because he "liked his Catholic-based social conservative values."

Mr. Flaherty lost that campaign to Ernie Eves, whose cabinet he then joined. Eves was defeated as premier by Dalton McGuinty in 2003, and Jim Flaherty again went for the leadership in 2004. Again, his friend Charles McVety supported him. In August of that year, Flaherty said, "My policy is that I'm in favour of the traditional definition of marriage—one man and one woman. I think it supports the family, which is the foundation of our society. I'm not opposed to the use of the notwithstanding clause in limited circumstances."

In May of 2004, nine thousand people attended a pro-marriage, family values rally on the lawn of Queen's Park, organized by firebrand and immensely impressive orator-minister Rev. Tristan Emmanuel. Speakers included Charles McVety, Jim Flaherty, Joseph Ben-Ami, and Saskatchewan Conservative MP and pastor Maurice Vellacott.

Four days before the convention vote, members of the Ontario PC party received the previously mentioned email from McVety, headed "How to Vote to Protect Marriage." "In order to defeat the pro-same-sex marriage candidate John Tory," it read, "either Frank Klees or Jim Flaherty will need to win. Each of Flaherty or Klees have considerable support in the leadership contest, and so it is important that every pro-marriage voter considers one of these two for their first choice and the other for their second choice."

The email caused controversy among PC members, since third-party organizations, like McVety's Canada Christian College, were banned from having internal party membership lists—a breach of the party's privacy policy. It was never publicly determined which camp—

Klees or Flaherty—had leaked the information to McVety.

After his loss to Tory, who won a seat in the legislature in March 2005, Flaherty quit to plan his entry into federal politics. Following the defection of Belinda Stronach from the Stephen Harper caucus, and the failed attempt by the Conservatives to defeat the government of Paul Martin, reports surfaced that Flaherty was plotting to unhorse Harper.

The heavily used news website Bourque posted that "longtime Ontario Cabinet Minister and two-time provincial leadership contender Jim Flaherty may well be positioning himself for an early opportunity to unseat Stephen Harper, the disappointing Conservative Party incumbent, increasingly seen as a lame duck leader whose political capital may well have expired with his botched handling of the recent national antagonism towards the long-government Liberals. . . . Failed retail heiress Nicky Eaton hosted a swish gathering at her country estate in Caledon for Flaherty's intimates to discuss a bid for Harper's job. Present and accounted for included Tony Clement . . . and Tom Long."

Five weeks before the January federal election in which Flaherty would win his seat in Whitby-Oshawa, he and neighbouring Conservative candidate and Charles McVety employee Rondo Thomas attended a seminar sponsored by the Canada Family Action Coalition and the Institute for Canadian Values, headed by Joseph Ben-Ami. The speaker, Ralph Reed, billed as a senior advisor to George W. Bush's election campaign, presented on winning elections. At that time he said, "We're not trying to change a church into a political party, and we're not trying to change a political party into a church, but if the people of the church don't get involved, somebody else will." Besides Mr. Flaherty and Mr. Thomas, also in attendance were Stephen Harper's Conservative candidates for Pickering-Scarborough East, Don Valley West, and York Centre.

On February 6, 2006, Jim Flaherty was named as finance minister of Canada by Prime Minister Stephen Harper, along with his provincial leadership supporter, John Baird, and his alleged federal leadership conspirator Tony Clement. The anti-abortion group Campaign Life applauded the cabinet, pointing out that a third of its members were active supporters. They include Agriculture Minister Chuck Strahl, Justice Minister Vic Toews, Fisheries Minister Loyola Hearn, Citizenship Minister Monte Solberg, House Leader Rob Nicholson, Security Minister Stockwell Day, Natural Resources Minister Gary Lunn, Revenue Minister Carol Skelton, and Finance Minister Jim Flaherty. Almost immediately, Ottawa was laced again with rumours that Mr. Flaherty was positioning himself to be the next leader of the Conservative Party of Canada.

In caucus Mr. Flaherty never spoke of his social conservative views. There is no evidence that his abrupt and substantial change in behaviour towards me was related to my growing adversarial relationship with his friend and political supporter, Charles McVety. However, Jim Flaherty did figure prominently in the days leading to my removal from caucus.

The pre-budget opus Mr. Flaherty was given in March spoke extensively of the need to reform the tax system to make it more family-friendly. A key proposal was the establishment of a family tax return, something first offered in my 1993 Progressive Conservative leadership campaign. This would allow income-splitting between spouses, a simple act that would nonetheless revolutionize how Canadians are taxed. The report also recommended retired couples be allowed to average out pension income between them for tax purposes, as a first step to full income-sharing.

While I needed no encouragement to fight for income-splitting, during the months of door-knocking that preceded the 2006 election this was, hands down, the number-one policy initiative that people were asking for. After the election, that theme was echoed in a series of Town Hall meetings, and then in the flood of pre-budget correspondence from taxpayers across the country. If the middle class could have had one single thing given to them by the new Stephen Harper administration, this was it.

My report made that clear. Income-splitting would not only end the unfairness between how single-income and dual-income families are taxed, it would improve the cash flow for most middle-income households, establish a monetary value for the unpaid work done by caregivers, remove a disincentive for some people to have children, allow others the option of providing care for the elderly or disabled, and give stay-at-home workers the ability to make RRSP contributions, since they would finally have earned income. Mr. Flaherty, I urged, do it.

But he did not. The May 2006 budget was silent on this issue.

A group of seniors activists approached me after having heard of my position, and asked for help in promoting the splitting of pension income between retired couples. It was agreed this could be a useful first step on the path to income-splitting for all couples, as is the case in several countries, including the United States and France. A background paper from the Library of Parliament was commissioned and I started work on a private member's bill on pension-splitting.

It then occurred to me that staging a national conference on the issue on Parliament Hill would be an effective and dramatic way of raising the profile of an issue that had, to date, received virtually no media or public attention. This was also a lobbying technique that had been used well in the past. As a Mulroney-era member of Parliament, I had convened such a conference in December of 1992 on restoring property rights in the Canadian Constitution, and invited stakeholders from across the country to attend. As a direct result of that event, and subsequent group actions, the Charlottetown Accord on constitutional reform embraced this key change, as well as granting Quebec "distinct society" status. The accord was subsequently defeated in a dramatic national referendum in 1993, with the "no" forces led by Reform Party leader Preston Manning.

Why not give pension-splitting a similar shot in the arm in 2006? The seniors' advocates agreed, and we spent the next four months planning the volunteer event for October 3 in the opulent Room 200 of the West Block. By the autumn, the group had expanded to represent more than 2.4 million seniors, and our media releases were generating positive news stories and columns in mainstream publications like the *National Post* and the *Toronto Star*. Suddenly pension-splitting had become a sexy issue, and our October event looked like it would garner the attention of a large number of MPs looking to be on the right side of it.

The momentum, however, would encounter a series of obstacles within the Conservative caucus and, especially, from Jim Flaherty. In advance of the summer caucus retreat in early August, my office asked for pension-splitting to be included on the agenda, and at 3 p.m. on Thursday, August 3, in a meeting room at the Nav Canada Conference Centre in Cornwall, I presented to Ontario caucus, asking for support. Most members were supportive, but not—as previously mentioned—MP Jeff Watson, who would soon lead my ouster from caucus, and not the minister of finance.

Mr. Flaherty spoke up, saying, "We have to be careful what we propose here, because there are other issues which have to be financed in the coming budget, and which have not yet been costed." He mentioned the Harper government promise of an additional 1 percent reduction in the GST, while I knew he was also absolutely certain to re-introduce the capital gains tax rollover promised in the election but, as yet, undelivered.

But Jim Flaherty did not stop there. "I'm also concerned about Garth Turner," he said, "and very concerned with this process."

It was a knife through the heart of the issue, the conference, and my lobbying within caucus. Flaherty's negativity shut down debate, and chair Gord Brown quickly canned the meeting. It was an echo of what was to come ten weeks later, on the day of my dismissal from the Conservative caucus when Mr. Flaherty stood and delivered a final blow. "I don't appreciate Garth Turner pushing things this government has not decided on," he said. "He is not running an alternative government."

Despite Cornwall, our coalition pressed ahead. As the date for the resumption of Parliament on September 18 approached, I wrote Rahim Jaffer, national Conservative caucus chair, and asked for a few minutes in the meeting that Wednesday morning to speak about pension-splitting and the October event. I was denied.

As it turned out, on that day—September 20—Essex MP Jeff Watson introduced his surprise motion in the early-morning Ontario caucus to have me removed, which led to the afternoon encounter in the cabinet committee room I have already described.

The pension-splitting conference proceeded, and was a Hill and media success. More than thirty members of Parliament attended, about a dozen of them brave Conservatives. The day before I had placed hand-addressed invitations on the desk of every MP in the House, the third invitation each had received. The day before, also, Jim Flaherty seemed determined to destroy the entire effort.

At a hastily arranged media scrum, Mr. Flaherty made the surprise statement that pension-splitting "is not a high priority, I can tell you that." He told reporters there was no way a form of income-splitting would take precedence over the deferring of capital gains, and, "in terms of taxing on a family basis and income-splitting, that's something we can work on over time."

Of course, the minister of finance had every right to make those comments, exercise caution, and dampen expectations. But he picked a curious time to do it, clearly and deliberately signalling to the media that the event about to happen was marginal and would be ignored by the Stephen Harper government. I was not surprised at Jim Flaherty's preoccupation with the capital gains tax cut, since Mr. Harper himself had told me over dinner at 24 Sussex two months earlier he "couldn't wait" to eliminate that tax. But I did not expect our event, now telegraphed to every seniors' group and pension organization in Canada, to be so boldly kneecapped.

But Flaherty was not done yet.

On September 25, the request was made of the minister of finance by me to ask a question of him during Question Period on October 3. My intent was to follow up on the pension-splitting conference, which would be held the day before, and to keep advancing the issue. I was well aware the question would be a "lob," and that his answer would be completely non-committal. But, as a lobbying MP, it was important to keep the pressure on as best I could in the House of Commons.

Every day Parliament is in session, forty-five minutes are devoted to Question Period. The Speaker allocates questions on the basis of a formula worked out by the parties, and each day there are three single queries allocated to members of the government Conservative caucus. These question slots, while set aside for backbench MPs to speak on behalf of constituents, are controlled by the party whip, the ministers, and the PMO. No Conservative MP is allowed to stand and put a question unless it has been approved in advance by the prime minister's office and the minister, whose answer must also be approved. In addition, the answer to the question must be rehearsed by the minister during the daily practice period, which takes place from 12:30 p.m. to 1:30, and is overseen by PMO officials.

In contrast, once I became an independent member of Parliament after October 19, 2006, I dealt directly with the Speaker and the Clerk of the House of Commons, and was able to ask questions each week, without informing anyone in advance of the content.

I made four requests for the right to question Mr. Flaherty before receiving an email from Candace Smith, the minister's director of parliamentary affairs: "Send me the question." In response, the following question was sent: "Representatives of two million pensioners met in Ottawa this week to back the concept of pension-splitting among retired couples. Does the minister understand their concerns for this tax fairness and is he prepared to address them in his coming budget?"

It was understood, of course, Flaherty would not answer the question, or give any indication of what he was, or was not, considering for the next budget. The answer I'd expect would be "I thank my honourable friend for his questions, and I know he has put considerable work into this issue. The security of seniors' incomes is of vital importance to this government, as Budget 2006 demonstrated, and these Canadians can rest assured we will constantly give them reasons to support this administration, as opposed to the former government, which ignored them for thirteen long years."

Will that, I thought, be too much to ask? And it was.

After Question Period on the day before the pension conference, and three hours before Mr. Flaherty would convene his media scrum to try to kill the issue, I received this email from my Hill office:

Hi Garth. I spoke to Candace Smith (Parliamentary Relations Directorate) from Minister Flaherty's office who has informed me that you will not be able to ask your question tomorrow during QP. I asked why not and was told that the Minister himself has denied you the opportunity to ask the question.

I then called Candace Smith, and asked directly for a reason. "Because," I was told by the staffer, "you can't."

It was now sixteen days before my suspension from the Conservative team. While that event was unknown yet, the futility of being a

Stephen Harper MP was not. Caucus members wanting to gain influence had been instructed to value discipline above all, not to speak to the media, not to try to influence government decisions, and not to question the impact on constituents, on penalty of expulsion. Additionally, my efforts to represent voters in the budget process had ended in disappointment and professional disaster while the attempt to lobby for pension-splitting on behalf of seniors was quashed.

There was no support to engage Canadians in a policy debate, or make the government look open and inclusive. Additionally, sadly, my voice in the House of Commons was silenced. At the same time, at the Cornwall caucus the PMO had instructed Conservative MPs to view their all-party committee work as nothing but support for ministers and government positions, while caucus members had been told they could not table any private members' bills that had not been approved, or even make one-minute statements in the Commons whose scripts had not been sanctioned.

While many of my colleagues—perhaps all of them—were willing to abide by these rules, I was not. The people of my riding had not sent me to Ottawa to be silent, to value advancing in caucus ahead of advancing a cause, or to bow to the instructions of a staffer. With each day that passed, each caucus meeting, each new restriction, instruction, directive, ban, and rule, my ability to function as a member of Parliament and to fulfill the expectations of the voters was being destroyed. Several times I said to my wife that if the voters ever really, truly knew what their MP had become, they would scoff.

I had gone to these stone castles in January with such high expectations. I drove up the 416 now each Sunday night with sadness and dread.

It was ironic that twelve days after I was banned from being a Conservative MP, Ottawa adopted the policy of pension-splitting, at the same time it broke an election promise not to tax income trusts. That night, Minister Flaherty's government said, "We are introducing a major positive change in tax policy for pensioners. We will permit income-splitting for pensioners beginning in 2007. This will significantly enhance the incentives to save and invest for family retirement security."

I sent an email to the groups that worked to achieve this. "We won," it read. Then I called Dorothy, and she yelled, "Congratulations!"

"Hey," I rused, "piece of cake."

I hung up the phone and stared over my laptop at the wall of the Ottawa condo. Above the desk was a large engraving of Centre Block, looking at the Library of Parliament from across the river. I'd bought it when I was an MP seventeen years earlier, and always found it majestic and inspiring. I'd looked at it often and thought of the time, as a sixteen-year-old, I'd hitchhiked to Ottawa, talked my way into John Diefenbaker's office during the flag debate, and ended up eating lunch with him in the parliamentary restaurant. The old man was monumental. Some day, I knew, I'd march into those buildings as a member and serve my country as he had.

I got up and walked to the Peace Tower.

Days earlier Flaherty had told my colleagues I should be tossed for pushing a policy he'd just adopted. Had he known it at the time? Maybe I belonged in the digital world. This one was a disaster.

CHAPTER SIX

"Quite the little shit disturber."

—Michael Wilson, Canadian ambassador to the United States

THE CAUCUS ROOM HAS TWO DOORS; the outer one wood, the inner one skinned in leather. No sound gets out. Like Vegas, what happens here stays here. It's a cardinal rule in politics, as long as you hold the power.

This book opens the door. It's not done lightly. I've been a federal politician, off and on, for nine years. It never crossed my mind to break this rule, until it was shattered for me.

The mainstream, modern, and moderate Conservative party that many people voted for last time is anything but. In reality, its caucus room is permeated with a kind of old-time religious fervour completely at odds with contemporary Canada. Worse, true power is not even being exercised by the people you elect, but by unaccountable backroomers who have the ear of an iron-spined prime minister consumed with gaining more power in the next vote.

On Wednesday, October 18, 2006, I flipped on the TV in my downtown Ottawa condo to watch myself being thrown out of my party, live on national news. There was Rahim Jaffer, the thirty-five-year-old MP and Harper-appointed national Conservative caucus chair giving a media scrum. It was obviously approved by the PMO's communications director Sandra Buckler, since everything was. Mr. Jaffer was telling reporters what had just happened in caucus. And, unfortunately, what he said was not accurate.

"This is not something that one person has felt. There were attacks that were made on individuals, including the prime minister, on his blog at different times. The theme of confidentiality was not being respected, in their opinion, and it restricted the ability for members to operate in a confidential way."

As CTV reported, "The decision was brought unanimously by the party's Ontario caucus Wednesday morning, Jaffer said. Although it came as a surprise, he said it was endorsed unanimously by the national caucus."

In politics, your word is your currency. Lose it, you're broke. Mr. Jaffer, who once sent a parliamentary aide to impersonate himself on a live radio show, dishonoured me in a profound way that day. But his comments also lifted the veil on a government, a leader, and a party that I found operates as much as a cult as a democratic representative body. And they hate the unfettered populist free-for-all of blogs, which is why no Conservative MP dared have one—other than the apparently suicidal Garth Turner. The charges Jaffer brought were as hollow and manipulative as those of Stephen Harper telling seniors, "We will never tax your income trusts."

Experiences have led me to a point I never expected to reach, and to tell you things you were never intended to hear. Caucus confidentiality is breached on a weekly basis in Ottawa, usually by the PMO. A Tory MP can be sent to tell the media other MPs were crying with gratitude for the PM behind those doors, and there are no consequences. The media reports it as fact. In contrast, my own party threatened me with expulsion two months earlier for mentioning that a topic—gun control—had been discussed in caucus.

"Confidentiality" was cited by Rahim Jaffer for expelling me from a party I'd served all my life and had once been a candidate to lead. But at the same time, "caucus confidentiality" was used as the reason that evidence of my breaking the confidentiality rule would not be presented. When it serves those in power to uphold a rule, it's a rule. When the rule's an impediment, it's a guideline.

For the record—as blogged—I never did "attack" the prime minister. Mr. Harper is a talented man trying his best to accomplish those goals that motivate him. I never set out to breach the confidence of people in the caucus room, and still believe that never happened, certainly not to the extent the PMO itself regularly does.

My caucus colleagues, nonetheless, never voted unanimously to expel me from their fold, as many confessed to me in the months to follow. "Nobody told us anything specifically about you, or what you had done, in that meeting," a former colleague told me, far from the Hill. "We just didn't know. And there was no vote." And the incident was a surprise to nobody involved, save me. It was a set-up.

Given these facts, I decided, reluctantly, to share with Canadians what's behind those doors. The damage inflicted on my career was, they hoped, irreparable. Given the lie that was broadcast across the country, there'll never be another caucus room I enter that someone does not wonder.

But how can one be surprised? When I joined Stephen Harper's party, now dressed in the respectability of the Conservative brand, it was quickly apparent Canadians had been conned. When confronted with the choice of saying what Mr. Harper wanted or telling the truth, I chose the latter. In doing so, I countered the most powerful man in the country and the ruthless crew around him.

Blameless? I'm far from it, and many of my former colleagues hate me. Through the blog, webcasting, and the mainstream media, over the course of ten crucial months, I spoke to voters as I believed a member of Parliament should—engaging them in issues, asking for input, raising questions, and trying to influence my own government's agenda according to the wishes of the people. This earned me the title from critics of media whore, and the pro-Harper trolls who police the blogosphere saw me as an egomaniac who couldn't get over being left out of cabinet. Then ultimately, when that didn't resonate with Canadians, I was a caucus cheat. That's a rap you don't beat.

The day the ouster happened, I asked people to look at all my words since being elected—all published—and find the caucus leak. The challenge was gleefully taken up by Stephen Harper supporters. One Tory blogger and self-proclaimed pundit, Stephen Taylor, told his readers he'd hit pay dirt. He pointed to an article I had written and posted five months earlier, saying an earlier, deleted version of that piece had mentioned a few moments of a caucus meeting.

"I have found a section which has been altered," Taylor wrote in a posting that exploded across the Internet. He cited my original version, in which I wrote about the coming multi-billion-dollar compensation for aboriginal Canadians affected by residential schools.

It wasn't too long ago that Indian Affairs Minister Jim Prentice took the podium in national caucus to brief people on the soon-to-be-announced settlement for aboriginal people victimized by their residential schools experience. Prentice apparently had been appalled at the deal ... still when he announced the multi-billion dollar amount involved, the room let out one collective gasp.

Then Taylor ran this, the altered post:

It wasn't long ago that Indian Affairs Minister Jim Prentice took over the highly complex issue of compensation for aboriginal people victimized by their residential schools experience. ... Still, it's a multi-billion dollar deal—simply breathtaking ...

Said Stephen Taylor: "I have presented an example of that breach here and hope it sheds some light into the legitimate concern of members of the Ontario Tory members [sic] that they might have one day fell [sic] victim to Garth's caucus gossip on his blog if they continued to meet with him in a forum of confidence."

Was this the best evidence of my crime, saying Prentice had briefed caucus on the prime issue his department faced, and that Liberal largesse was found surprising? In any case, I sent Taylor an email telling him the day I wrote that first post, chief government whip Jay Hill called me and asked if I would alter the words to remove the reference to caucus. Of course, I said, and I did. Why not cooperate? After all, the whip didn't order me to remove the post, or shut down the blog, or get with the program, or shut up—he just asked that two sentences be changed. And they were.

During the 2005–6 election campaign, on two occasions the Conservative war room called me to ask that photos of Stephen Harper—previously published in the conventional media—be removed from the blog. They were. It happened again in September 2006, when Jim Flaherty approached me in caucus and complained bitterly about a picture of himself published on the blog that morning. He thought the shot, taken by a Canadian Press photographer, was puffy and unflattering. It was replaced within fifteen minutes with a picture of a smiling, thinner, paternalistic-looking minister of finance.

There was only one demand ever from anyone in the Conservative Party that my blog go dark. That was made by the prime minister's chief of staff, Ian Brodie, immediately after floor-crossing Liberal David Emerson was appointed to the federal cabinet. But by then, it was too late.

Did I cross the line as an MP? After all, an experienced member of Parliament like me should have known what to expect from a party, a PMO, a caucus, and a prime minister. You can judge for yourself, of course. It's all online.

But caucus confidentiality was likely never the issue. Instead, being booted out had much more to do with the difference between an institution Canadians knew by its storied name, the Conservative Party, and the one they ended up electing, the Stephen Harper Party— and what I had to say about it. The vehicle for that, of course, was the blog. A digital demon feared on Parliament Hill in the months following the Harper ascent.

During the 2006 election, Conservative campaign commander Doug Finley was obsessed with presenting Canadians messages of a moderate party with a reasonable, hockey dad leader, while keeping extremist candidates under wraps. For that reason, for example, Canada Christian College pastor Rondo Thomas, running in Ajax-Pickering, was assigned his own media handler, while controversial evangelical candidates like David Sweet in Hamilton and Harold Albrecht in Kitchener were sometimes hidden during media events. Reporters were physically removed at a Mississauga rally before televangelists Charles McVety and David Mainse arrived for a private audience and prayer with Stephen Harper.

Finley's communications team routinely engaged in manipulation of the media, putting up spokespeople they knew would present a moderate face, like future Heritage Minister Bev Oda, while keeping the availability of others that networks had requested under wraps. After the 2004 campaign in which rogue candidate comments were made on abortion and same-sex marriage, Finley determined that the face of the Conservative Party would be one that reflected the mainstream, secular, middle-class soccer moms whose votes were being courted.

As a candidate in that election, I would be welcomed as a part of that marketing effort. An example: One week before the January 23 vote I tromped around a Burlington suburb with Rick Bell, political columnist for the *Calgary Sun*, from Stephen Harper's hometown. This was very much the battleground for the Canadian middle-class voter so coveted by both the Conservatives and Liberals. This riding had been held by the Grits for thirteen years with the last Tory to hold it being, ironically, me—when I was unceremoniously dumped as the Reform Party split the right-centrist vote down the middle. On the western fringe of urban Toronto, Halton represented a beachhead into the metrosexual marketplace and its vote-rich forty-three ridings.

Doug Finley was informed of the Bell incursion east, and read—
without comment—the following account, published on the blog on
January 15:

Rick Bell is the kind of reporter you'd expect to walk out of a bad
1940s movie. He's self-possessed, cocky, amusing, forceful and
very much a character. If he were not dressed in a parka and a
toque with a cellphone today, you could easily picture him in a
trench coat and fedora with a flash bulb-toting twenty-pound
camera slung over his shoulder.

He's a columnist with the *Calgary Sun*, making big headlines
out west these days. His assignment: travel east to the 905 belt of
Ontario, and report back to Albertan readers on why we Ontari-
ans are suddenly feeling inclined to vote for Conservatives. He
was sent to visit Liberal-held ridings which, in his estimation, are
about to go blue. So, he called me.

Bell is also interested in what being a Conservative means in
places like Halton, as opposed to a place like Calgary where, of
course, the Reform movement was born. He seemed intrigued
when we spoke about the message that candidates like me are
giving voters, and questioned me closely about what it is that folks
in Halton care about.

Simple, I said. People here are not angry, alienated or out to
foment revolution. Instead, they are looking for a positive
change—better government, more honest and forthright leaders,
way more accountability, and people in charge who understand
what a middle-class family needs and wants. How hard is it to
talk about those things, and set out to achieve them? Stable mortgage rates. Lower personal taxes. A child care plan. Assured health
care. Fairer family taxes. Tougher laws to curb crime. Help for
investors, small businesses and seniors.

So, Rick, I said, it has little to do with the Conservative-

Liberal-Reform thing. People in Halton are not by nature partisans or ideologues. Support for Liberals here has been wide and very shallow, and voters are quite receptive to Conservatives with decent platforms which resonate with them, so long as they can be assured the party is modern. That means open, inclusive, mainstream, tolerant, and small-c fiscally conservative without obsessing over social issues.

Not a day goes by now, I told the Cowboy, that I do not speak to many Liberals who want an alternative, who love our policies and approach to government, who are truly ready for a change— and who also want some assurance that Conservative does not mean Reform. And that is exactly what I give them. It is exactly what I believe.

Show me, the buckaroo said. So off we went to Burlington to knock on doors on one of the dwindling number of streets I have never before walked upon—this one being Butternut Crescent.

We piled out of the truck, went to the odd side of the street and started knocking. The first woman to answer called me by name, was polite and friendly, and Rick was impressed. The second doorbell yielded a woman who also knew me, and called out to her husband in another room. "Come in," she said. "He wants to meet you."

The guy was lying prone on the floor, covered with a blanket, head propped on a pillow. He reached up and shook my hand and started talking about the Conservative platform. Turns out he's a worker at Ford in Oakville and was nursing a pinched nerve in his back. He pledged complete support to me and ordered a lawn sign, which I hammered in on our way out.

Outside we headed to the next door, only to be stopped by a minivan in the middle of Butternut. The driver called me from his open window, said he had missed me when I canvassed his house, asked for a brochure, shook my hand, and said he would be voting Conservative. Behind me I could feel Rick's incredulous breath on the back of my neck.

"You script this?" he asked.

Over the next ninety minutes we did about sixty-five houses. We were invited inside a few times. I signed autographs for some children. We were greeted with familiarity, respect, thanks, and almost a kind of relief. "Since 1973," a man told me in his foyer as his wife looked on, "you are the first politician who has ever knocked on my door." I thought about the past twelve years, eleven of which one Liberal had represented this couple, and never met them.

"I said to The Wife," he continued, "that I was going to vote for the first guy who showed up, who cared to show up." And The Wife said, laughing, "Thank God it was you!"

Odd side done, halfway back down the even side, Rick said he had seen enough. We had encountered no Liberals, had chalked up at least a dozen new supporters, and counted almost everyone else as a likely or accessible supporter. Rick called me a couple of hours later from his hotel room on the 401 in Cambridge.

"I've got my lead," he said. "It'll be, 'No doubt about it, the Conservatives are winning on Butternut Crescent.'" And he was gone.

Over and over and over again, this was the message my team and I delivered to the doors of thousands of people who had not voted Conservative for almost a generation. And, consistently, we would encounter people who said, "Well, you seem like a good guy and I like what I hear, but that Stephen Harper scares the crap out of me. He's so, you know, Reform." And I would repeat the mantra that Rick Bell heard on every stoop: we are modern, open, inclusive, mainstream, tolerant, and small-c fiscally conservative, without obsessing over social issues. If I thought it were different, I said, if I thought Stephen

Harper was an extremist, then as a Progressive Conservative MP who represented you before, I would not be standing here at your door. Trust me. I know what you want.

And then I told people their income trust investments were safe, simply because Stephen Harper said they would be. In Town Hall meetings and in a living room full of skeptics in suburban Oakville one memorable campaign night I gave personal assurances our party was principled, democratic, grassroots, and would never endorse a floor-crossing traitor. I repeated my position against reopening the same-sex marriage debate, and took a lot of slammed doors in the nose from people who thought Mr. Harper was an intolerant homophobe. I'd knock on those doors again, and say, judge us by our actions—this is a party where the safety zone exists between religion and politics. You'll see. Trust me. I know what you want.

And they did. I won.

On election night, as the new Conservative MP, I wrote this:

Now the next voyage begins. A minority government in which every MP will be a precious commodity. A contentious, policy-filled agenda and a leader and a party that promised real change. Here in Halton, lots of people—thousands of them—who this time switched their votes from Liberal to Conservative, in part because I assured them they were voting for an alternative that was modern, credible, tolerant and open. Man, this is going to be interesting.

It certainly was. Less than ten months later, I was no longer a member of the team, ousted for breaking confidentiality rules that had never been in jeopardy and for telling secrets that never were. My accuser was an MP who came to national attention as a media fraud, and the "surprise" operation had the PMO's fingerprints all over it—Doug Finley's fingerprints.

Most worrisome, though, was my party. Far from being "modern, credible, tolerant, and open" it had turned out to be a narrow, dark, unhappy place where dissenting opinion was discouraged, then penalized, and where MPs were expected to be silent, subservient, and submissive. Caucus resembled a cult more than an open forum. Those few who asked questions or proffered ideas were silenced, shunned, and in my case, excommunicated.

In November of 2006, two weeks before the Liberals were to choose Stéphane Dion, one of the veterans of the Parliamentary Press Gallery looked at me over a plate of alfredo and said, "Harper's running out of cards to play. Conservatives desperately need to expand their base, and this constant catering to the fringe has to end."

He lit a cigarette on Sparks Street as we walked towards the Hill in a bitter wind. "In a few months, maybe sooner, you'll see [Jim] Prentice, [Peter] MacKay, and [Jim] Flaherty planting the seeds of their organizations. The knives will be out. Stephen Harper will never get a majority." He stopped, butted out in front of the media building, and turned. "Harper is fucked. You don't know how lucky you are."

But the day the caucus door shut behind me, luck seemed to be the last thing I had. The reality of being an independent member of Parliament was forced upon me in a rush. While Rahim Jaffer did not make his "surprise" announcement until after noon, by 2:15 p.m. the Speaker had managed to assign me another seat on the opposite side of the House, write a letter informing me, and have a new seating plan laid out and printed for MPs, the public galleries, the media, and the general public. "I wish to inform you that as of today, I have assigned you to seat number 279 in the House of Commons, as indicated on the seating plan attached," Peter Milliken wrote. Seat 279, I discovered, was the Outer Siberia of the Commons, the most remote point possible from Seat 11, the one occupied by Stephen Harper.

At the same time, 12:30 p.m., the House of Commons IT department called me on my BlackBerry to inform me that the computers in my Hill and riding offices would be shut down. "Why?" I asked. "Because we were told to reconfigure your mail settings." I was being disconnected from the Conservative server, and the techs told me they'd had written instructions given to them by the chief government whip "earlier today."

The consequences were starting to sink in. I was off the House of Commons Finance Committee, turfed in the middle of critical pre-budget consultations. The tens of thousands of dollars my campaigning had raised for the next election were gone—now the property of the Conservative Party. Within days I'd be banned by some party official I'd never heard of from ever running again as a Tory, a completely unexpected act of vindictiveness. And I'd have to return to my riding and explain how it was the voters sent me to Ottawa as a Conservative, and I came back as something else.

But that was not all of the explaining to be done. There was also the disappearance of the modern party I had pitched in order to win this seat in the first place. This was far more about the voters than about one MP. I was just the representative of the people but, as such, what happened to me also happened to them. Their party had also left town.

How had this happened?

How had things gone so wrong within a caucus and a government that had had so much hope? Stephen Harper had promised a new dawn of openness, transparency, and accountability and yet ended up refusing to tell his own MPs when he brought in deep cuts to program spending; threatening caucus members with suspension if they talked to the media without permission; refusing to consult with his own intergovernmental minister before recognizing the Quebecois as a nation; using closure to cut off debate in the House of Commons; raising government spending to a historic high and raising income taxes in his very first budget; revoking Commons approval of senior appointments when his first one was rejected by MPs; breaking a promise and taxing trust investments without consultation or warning; presiding over a party that provoked an RCMP raid on party headquarters; appointing two people to cabinet never elected as Conservatives and one never elected at all; and, of course, busting me.

Every week that I was a Stephen Harper Conservative it became more difficult to return to my riding, hold Town Hall meetings, and defend the latest developments. While Mr. Harper's government was acting decisively on budget matters, Afghanistan, softwood lumber, and a host of other issues, it was increasingly seen by my constituents as remote and narrow.

Of course, these folks did not know the actual situation—the influence of the righteous Right on Conservative politicians and policies, and the utter disdain showed by the prime minister, his cabinet, or the hired guns in the PMO for what grassroots Canadians actually thought, or wanted.

And it was this distancing from the people—those in my riding who had made such a leap of faith to cast their ballots for Conservatives and for Mr. Harper—that I found most troubling. It was this communications gulf I most wanted to bridge. Knocking on all those doors for all those months tends to turn anyone into a democrat. It certainly worked on me. I owed them after January 23. And I wasn't going to let them down.

One vital way of staying in touch with my constituents—and by this time the constituency seemed to stretch across the entire country—was the blog. What had started as a valuable tool in winning an election, by being able to instantly communicate with a growing digital audience, became a force of its own. Monthly audiences grew from a couple of hundred thousand before the election to between one and a half and two million consistently after becoming an MP. The blog was updated daily with original content, as I tried to write well-researched and reasoned pieces on what we were doing in Ottawa, and encouraged response.

Within weeks, scores of other sites linked to mine and sent bus-loads of visitors. Reporters would simply quote the blog within news stories, instead of actually interviewing me. My articles were routinely reprinted, then torn to shreds on pro-Harper, far-right sites like Free Dominion. Traffic spiked as high as a million hits a day, and the fact that an MP within Stephen Harper's caucus would carry on such a public dialogue itself became an issue.

Meanwhile, as the weeks and months of the self-named "Canada's New Government" rolled by, there was no choice in my mind but to write and speak in defence of the principles I had cam-paigned on—the basis of what had been sold as the Conservative Party. What those Canadian voters wanted. Tolerant, open, mainstream, inclusive, modern.

This decision would be fatal.

In the end, lots of people have said, the blog brought me down. Around the world, I was held up as the greatest example of a "dooced politician"—a person who had lost his job because of his website. When Rahim Jaffer waded into the post-caucus cameras, he said exactly that: "There were attacks that were made on individuals, including the prime minister, on his blog at different times."

But blogging was not the crime, just as revealing mythical caucus secrets wasn't it, either. Actually, I don't even think the dissing of some of my colleagues for their narrow, disturbing views or intolerant beliefs was the cause of the fate that befell me. No, it was far more consequential than that.

The people who populate Canada's New Government promised one thing and have delivered another. They preached openness and have closed their ranks. They promised transparency and yet operate in secret. They said they'd be accountable yet have no interest in lis-tening. They said they'd be tolerant yet punish dissenters. While a cau-cus room should be a place of vigorous debate and hard-won consensus, this one's a sanctuary where the converted gather.

The prime minister is a man who knows what he wants and is working hard to achieve it. Self-motivated and self-sufficient, he does not ask for advice from those the voters sent to Ottawa, simply because it's not required. For him, democracy's only messy when it's uncontrolled. And who wants a mess in caucus?

On the night of September 18, 2006, somebody set Jim Hawkes's house on fire. The former Conservative MP's home in the Varsity district of Calgary escaped destruction when the blaze, which had been set on his welcome mat, was extinguished and ended up toasting the front door.

When I saw Jim a few days later in the grounds of 24 Sussex as part of a former parliamentarians association event, he was still shaken. "It really rattles you," he said, "and I'm too old for this stuff now." Hawkes was the chief government whip for Brian Mulroney's Progressive Conservative government during the first years I sat in the House of Commons. He hired a young Stephen Harper to work on his staff. Eventually Harper turned and ran against his old boss as the Reform Party candidate, knocking him off.

The morning after the fire, Hawkes told the Calgary media exactly what he thought: the fire was deliberately set. Not only that, but he said he knew who did it: renegade supporters of current Conservative MP Rob Anders who were offended over a lawsuit Hawkes and ten other people had launched against the Calgary West riding association of the Conservative Party of Canada. It was a warning, he said.

"It just stinks," he told me, as we stood under the party tent between the shrimp table and Laureen Harper in a Calgary Flames hockey sweater, "that we even need to fight for democracy." In fact, what happened in Calgary West provides an interesting glimpse into the current Stephen Harper machine, the one that uses rules when they are most convenient.

Rob Anders is a five-time Conservative member of Parliament, committee chairman, worker in Stephen Harper's leadership campaigns, and an early adopter of the Reform movement. He was an active Reform member on campus at the University of Calgary, and went on to work with the National Citizens' Coalition, where Mr. Harper was in charge, directing a lobby group called Canadians Against Forced Unionism.

Mr. Anders made national headlines in 2001 when Parliament conferred citizenship upon former South African president Nelson Mandela, whom the Calgary MP called "a Communist and a terrorist." Mr. Anders held up unanimous consent in the House for the honour, then refused to take Mandela's phone call when he reached out to make peace.

Rob Anders is a member of the National Firearms Association, the Responsible Firearms Owners of Alberta, and the religious-based lobby groups Focus on the Family and Canada Family Action Coalition (supported by televangelist Charles McVety). Said the *Calgary Herald* in April 2002, "That a fringe character such as Anders is still active in the new party should be a red flag for those who want the Conservatives to move to the centre.... The Conservative Party can become a national alternative to the Liberals, but Harper will need the courage to tell old friends who have stood by him their time in the spotlight is over."

But, apparently, not yet. Since 2004 there has been an active push within Calgary West to find another Conservative candidate, which Mr. Anders has been able to resist, and which came to a head in August 2006 with the potential candidacy of Walter Wakula. But this long-time Tory was thwarted by the national party's strict application of new nomination rules, designed by Doug Finley and approved just days before. Mr. Wakula (and the rest of the riding) was informed on the Friday night of a long weekend that the nomination meeting would take place in thirty days (on the eve of the next long weekend).

Thus, an Anders contender had just nine days to sign up new members, apply to be a candidate, and come up with a financial bond and successful police background check. As it was impossible to pull off, Wakula and others gave up. Mr. Anders was acclaimed. Subsequently, Jim Hawkes and ten other local Conservatives, disgusted at the lack of grassroots democracy, launched a lawsuit against the party, claiming proper procedures were not followed, including having the nomination committee chaired by one of Anders's employees.

Commented Don Martin in the *Calgary Herald*, "This is but one riding example of the 308 where a party with populist roots has morphed into a governing force that uses strong-arm tactics to ensure the fix is in for its preferred public face."

Meanwhile, Mr. Anders was fighting another lawsuit from a former constituency office employee, James Istvanffy, who alleged he was fired after questioning the way Anders handled his finances. In his statement of claim, Istvanffy said the MP defrauded taxpayers and violated election laws by borrowing money from his staff for personal expenses, then paying them back with salary increases, false expense claims, and even by handing over government-owned furniture. He also alleged members of Anders's staff worked full-time on a Stephen Harper campaign while still pulling down House of Commons salaries, in contravention of the law.

In June 2007, federal Liberals made the most of the situation by calling for an RCMP investigation into Anders and the serious charge of defrauding taxpayers. Anders denied all allegations, saying he would vigorously defend himself. Eventually the parties reached a settlement, the terms of which were not revealed.

What does Rob Anders have to do with Garth Turner? It might go to the issue of how parties choose to operate and the standards of behaviour they apply. Mr. Anders called Nelson Mandela a terrorist; his tenure ignited a legal battle and, possibly, arson; he faced charges of defrauding the taxpayers; his case hit the floor of the House of

Commons; and opponents asked the RCMP to investigate. And the Conservative Party, by all accounts, took extraordinary measures to protect him.

Twenty feet from Jim Hawkes that September evening, towering over the crowd around him like an oak tree shading grateful cattle, was Michael Wilson. Unlike the former MPs invited to the prime minister's home because they used to be important, Wilson emanated power. Appointed by Stephen Harper to be the Canadian ambassador to the United States, moving in where Frank McKenna had moved out, Wilson was known to be the man behind the softwood lumber deal everyone else was taking credit for, including his boss.

For most of the years I was in the House, Wilson was the minister of finance, a hulking great grey god who withstood everything an angry nation could throw at him for inflicting the Goods and Services Tax upon it. He left politics intact, returned to Bay Street, and now was triumphant in his second coming upon the political stage.

Our relationship had been respectful and productive, mentor to apprentice, but started in a swirl of mistrust. As a tabloid newspaper daily columnist I'd called him "Mikey," pilloried his low-dollar policies, and rallied support against his crazy value-added tax scheme. Brian Mulroney had even called the publisher of the *Toronto Sun* to tell him to tell the editor to tell Turner to back off. I didn't.

So when I walked into the Conservative caucus room in 1988, Wilson had every reason to give me space. But he didn't, engaging me instead in the design and implementation of the GST itself, explaining his plan, its benefits and its consequences for the country, and turning me into an apostle. Ironically, I'd come to administer the thing.

The contrast with this day was not lost on him. "Well," Wilson said, looking down at me, "you've turned into quite the little shit disturber." And I got that Mike Wilson smile. "I'm happy you're still at it."

The conversation lasted just a few moments before Mrs. Harper arrived. Before she made it through a passing gaggle of MPs' wives, I asked for advice. "Be careful," Wilson said quietly. "He'll stop anyone he thinks is getting in the way of the majority."

A week after Jim Flaherty's first budget, three months after the government took office and a few days before the country would be shocked and the prime minister angered at a Canadian military death, I decided it was time to try to make this thing work. Ian Brodie and I had not spoken since the day he ordered me to shut down the blog, shut up, and support David Emerson. Even in national caucus, where he showed up every Wednesday, entering conspicuously through the doorway that, by unspoken convention, is reserved for the prime minister, the guy avoided my gaze. The cold war, obviously, had to end, or my days as a Conservative would be pointless.

The PMO switchboard put me through to voice mail. Brodie called back on his cellphone from Mexico, where Stephen Harper was meeting George Bush officially for the first time, to discuss the highly secretive SPP, Security and Prosperity Partnership. We should meet soon, I said, you and me and Sandra Buckler.

A week or so later my cowboy boots tromped up the worn stone steps of the Langevin Block on Wellington Street opposite Parliament Hill. Langevin was public works minister to Sir John A. Macdonald, and the guy who decided the growing Canadian government needed an office building.

Construction of the monolithic structure began in 1883, was finished six years later, and today is virtually unchanged from 120 years ago. I arrived at the spacious foyer with the dark brown granite pillars and massive, steep staircase draped in ornate, painted ironwork. I was stopped there, cold, by a wall of glass and two pass card-operated sliding glass doors watched over by a humourless security guard who couldn't care less that I was an MP. It took three calls to Ian Brodie's office before the transparent sea parted.

The inner sanctum is unexpectedly modest. There are Trudeau-era dangly overhead lights and a bilious colour of green on too many walls. The wide, second-floor corridor leading to the executive area is lined with the offices of senior PMO staffers—a fraction of the number who currently populate the prime minister's personal staff. Brodie's office, at least the one he met me in, is long, narrow, and unfriendly, dominated by a hulking radiator and, at this moment, Buckler.

Brodie waved me in and I sat beside Buckler on a couch that Public Works should have landfilled a decade ago. To say the meeting was strange would be an epic understatement. The prime minister's communications person sat there and stared into my ear for twenty minutes without saying anything, answering my comments, or making any attempt to thaw. It was a remarkable performance.

Harper's chief of staff was more talkative, but what I heard didn't have a shred of conciliation in it. This visit had been intended as a peace initiative, a visible symbol of my willingness to enter PMO turf, talk about the issues Mr. Harper was concerned about, and find a way forward. Surely, if the guys at the top of the political food chain were as smart as they must be, then they'd understand I was there to change the status quo. How hard would it be to tell The Big Guy that, you know, Turner came over and sat on my couch and asked what he might do to help our effort? After all, a reasonable manager would know it makes a hell of a lot more sense to have a dissident worker involved in a project than out stirring up shit in a nest of reporters.

So, I pitched him. Chair the House of Commons finance committee? After all this was my thing—had written books on it, done TV shows exploring it, lectured across Canada on it. Nope, Brodie said, forget it. Caucus would be against this—a strange response, when two-thirds of committee members belong to the opposition.

Maybe a special project then, something dear to our collective hearts as Conservatives? How about the restoration of property rights? My ear was getting frostbitten, as Brodie nixed that one, too. The prime minister will determine when the right time is to talk to you, he said, as he got up and paced.

I made a point then of saying I was not looking for a job, or asking for anything special to be conferred upon me. No title. No money. It just seemed that having a caucus member with cabinet experience, committee experience, MP experience, private sector experience, and some public profile sitting around was not the most productive use of resources.

Brodie ignored that. "You sure have gotten people riled up," he added. "You might be interested in knowing the PMO now has a Garth Turner correspondence unit." The tone was not encouraging, and I could only imagine the responses being turned out. Buckler blew her nose. She had a cold. I wondered how germs could survive in that climate.

Twenty minutes after it started, it was over. I went down the grand staircase, through the security checkpoint and back out into the weak spring sunshine. The foray had accomplished nothing. There would be no reconciliation. No attempt to find something to keep me busy, to keep me in the fold or redefine the relationship. It was clear at that moment that Brodie—and, by extension, Stephen Harper— had zero interest in finding common ground. My initial assessment of Harper was proving to be depressingly accurate—supremely self-possessed, driven by the unassailable correctness of his path and the knowledge he knew at all times what was best. Not a team leader interesting in building and inspiring the team, he was rather a leader by virtue of his superiority.

Mr. Harper's condescending treatment of those around him was best illustrated to me five months later when Michael Chong stood before reporters in the first-floor Centre Block news theatre and said four stunning words, "I was not consulted." The young intergovernmental affairs minister had resigned his cabinet post ninety minutes earlier, walking into House Leader Rob Nicholson's office and handing over his Question Period briefing books just before the daily session in the Commons.

It was the day of a historic debate and vote on the surprise motion the prime minister had popped on Parliament, recognizing "the Quebecois" as a nation within Canada. The move had come a day after Bloc Québécois leader Gilles Duceppe had tabled a motion that would have had Parliament declare Quebec a nation—a nation that would have been soundly trounced. But the prime minister, worried about his party's political future in that province and the negative signal that might have sent, quickly countered with his own version, adding the words "within a united Canada."

Suddenly the federal Parliament of Canada was being asked by the prime minister to support a motion declaring an ill-defined group of Canadians, "the Quebecois," as a nation-state within the country. Not only was the word "nation" not defined, but questions abounded over who actually were going to be granted nationhood. At a disastrous press conference hastily convened by Senator Marjory LeBreton and Transport Minister Lawrence Cannon, it was suggested that "Quebecois" included only francophone descendants of the first colonists of Lower Canada; then changed to include first nations; then amended again to include Lebanese-born immigrants to Montreal and anglophone government workers living in Aylmer.

Meanwhile the Bloc separatists who sat beside me in the House were telling me cheerfully that "Quebecois" really meant every person living in the province—so when MPs voted to make them a nation, it was actually endorsing the inevitable independent status of Quebec itself. "*C'est une bonne chose pour tous*," I heard. "*Votons!*"

This bothered me a lot, and I was one of only sixteen MPs who voted against a motion with undefined terms and unknown consequences. It bothered most Canadians, and it bothered Chong. He told his press conference he could not support any motion that encouraged "ethnic nationalism" in Canada, and that he must do the principled thing and resign, rather than vote in favour.

And he, like all Conservatives that night, was not given a choice. The Quebecois nation vote was "triple-lined" by chief government whip Jay Hill, which meant any Tory not supporting the prime minister would be kicked out of caucus and then the party, as I had been just days before. The only way Michael Chong, as a Harper minister, could avoid voting for the thing was to resign, then abstain. And he did. But before doing so, he revealed that Stephen Harper had not even spoken to him about the most important issue that could ever have affected his area of responsibility. Harper had quickly devised a strategy, determined it was correct, and then lined up the necessary opposition support to get it passed.

Twenty-four hours before the vote, I ran an online poll on my website asking for suggestions on how to vote. More than 70 percent of respondents were opposed to the nation motion, a result that was mirrored two days later in a national poll. Harper had brought in his nation-within-Canada idea without notice, and his government moved closure to cut off debate after just one day. Any MP who wanted to consult constituents was given a single weekend to do so, and for any Conservative member—being ordered to vote in favour regardless of public opinion—well, what was the point?

At eight minutes to three on the day the vote was scheduled to take place, I was sitting in the House, waiting to ask a question during Question Period. As usual—being an independent—my question would be last, just at three o'clock. I was planning to ask Citizenship

Minister Monte Solberg when he was going to address the issue of
dual citizenship, forcing expats to file annual income tax returns.

The Berry on my desk vibrated with an incoming call. I thought
about ignoring it, since the Speaker was less than four minutes away
from recognizing me, but instead answered and ducked behind the
curtain (not a difficult task where I happen to sit). It was Martin
O'Hanlon, of the Canadian Press. "We're hearing that Michael Chong
is going to resign," he said. "Can you help us with that. Is it true?"

No idea, I said, but I highly doubt it. I'll check.

Chong at that moment was my idea of a Stephen Harper boy
scout. I'd heard him defend the government with a perfect recitation
of Sandra Buckler talking points time and again, and he'd joined the
line of speakers in caucus two weeks earlier arguing for my sorry ass
to be parked outside the party. He was young, ambitious, thrust
unexpectedly into a cabinet role, and widely considered to be a rising
Tory star. How could the guy quit?

I called Esther, who got on the issue instantly and called me back
at 2:58 p.m. with a confirmation, from Chong's own constituency staff
whom he'd just told he was quitting over opposition to the Quebec
nation motion. I called O'Hanlon back with time to say, only, "Turn on
the TV." I was pocketing the phone when Speaker Milliken announced, "The Honourable Member for Halton."

So I turned and faced the prime minister across the floor, who
did not look at me—his habit with questioners—and said, "Mr.
Speaker, later today we are about to vote on the contentious issue of
declaring the Quebecois a nation. Will the prime minister update this
House on the apparent resignation of his intergovernmental affairs
minister, and will he withdraw this motion as a result?"

The House had gone completely silent, and I was aware of three
hundred faces looking at me as I finished my question, then swivelling
to Stephen Harper. He paused a small moment, put on a tight smile,
turned and faced the Speaker, and gave a statement defending his mo-

tion. Silence. Shock. Immediately interim Liberal leader Bill Graham shot to his feet and asked, directly, "Will the Right Honourable prime minister tell this House whether or not his minister has resigned?" And Stephen Harper did it again—standing, making a statement about Quebec, and not mentioning Chong. Apparently, he had already ceased to exist.

Outside in the foyer, a kind of stunned panic had set in. The news about Michael Chong had taken every reporter completely by surprise, and Mr. Harper's incredible refusal to confirm or deny it was causing utter confusion. I did some scrums, then sat on the bench there just watching a historic moment unfold. I also thought about Michael, and what an unfair opinion I had held of him. The guy had just done a courageous and democratic thing, eschewing title, money, and influence for principle and conviction. Instantly, he was the antithesis of all those Tories who in a few hours would vote for something profound, simply because they had been told.

As I sat there Susan Bonner came and sat beside me. "Well," she said, smiling, "that must have felt good." Susan had been covering my saga for CBC television's *The National* since February, when she did a piece on my rebel, anti-Emerson status and later reported on my caucus ouster. The irony of the moment—Garth Turner, punished, expelled, disenfranchised by Stephen Harper, calling the PM on his cabinet defection—was too much to ignore. Then her phone rang, and she tore off down the hall after a cameraman.

Truthfully, I tried to feel good. Sweet revenge? But it didn't work. It was just sad.

Michael Chong had willingly committed political suicide, making the ultimate choice you'd expect from a true representative of the people. And yet the prime minister didn't even have the decency to acknowledge his existence in the House of Commons, let alone the ultimate step he had taken. Less than an hour later, Chong would give a conciliatory, sympathetic, and sweet media conference in which he praised Stephen Harper, professed his faith and confidence in the Conservative government, and characterized his act as being a personal one, making no comment on his leader.

"The reason why I got involved in politics is my belief in this nation we call Canada. I believe in this great country of ours and I believe in one nation, undivided," he said. "This is a fundamental principle for me, not something on which I can or will compromise. Not now, not ever."

But he also said, "I was not consulted."

So, it was sad for Michael, since had I not asked my question his resignation wouldn't even have made it into Hansard. It was sad the prime minister had taken a unilateral decision with national implications and ignored his own cabinet in doing so. Chong's rational, fact-based, and sensible opinion on this needed to be heard.

It was sad the entire government caucus was ordered to support the government position, regardless of how they—representatives of the Canadian people—felt about something that could have profound consequences down the road. It was sad that public opinion, as expressed in the results of the online survey, placed on every MP's desk before the vote, was dismissed. It was sad that one Tory MP scrawled a message on the poll result and had a page bring it to back my desk. "SAVE YOUR PAPER," it said.

Most sad, however, was what the PMO then did to young, principled Michael Chong.

His destruction started the next day. The *Toronto Star* carried a story quoting unnamed sources (of course) saying Chong was not a team player because he didn't tell Harper soon enough of his reservations and quit too abruptly.

History was also quickly rewritten to suggest that Chong misspoke in his media conference when he said he was not consulted. The PMO spinners told the newspaper the PM talked to him about this at least twice over the summer. Most damning, the PMO insiders said—leaking confidential cabinet material to the media—that Michael went to QP briefing on the fateful day, practised answers to questions on the unity file, then shockingly handed in his briefing books to Nicholson, and walked.

Now, who would have details like that? Just other cabinet members and the PMO staff briefing them. Given the day, and the issue, this would likely have included senior people. In other words, here are the top operatives in Mr. Harper's inner circle leaking insider information to the media in a deliberate attempt to forever destroy the political career of a man who quit in the most gentle fashion, and for the right reasons.

Caucus confidentiality may be an inviolate rule, or it may be a guideline. Or more likely, it's just crap.

On Wednesday, May 17, 2006, at 6:55 p.m. local time in Ottawa, Senator Anne Cools was sitting in the off-white living room of 24 Sussex Drive, playing the piano. The chef was in the kitchen preparing Alberta beef and Atlantic salmon. Prime Minister Stephen Harper was in his third-floor Centre Block office being briefed. I was leaving my Hill office in the Justice Building. At that moment, 24 kilometres west of Kandahar City, Nichola Goddard, 26, was being shelled to death in an intense firefight.

The captain's death was the first-ever female combat fatality suffered by the Canadian Forces and it came on a hell of a day. The prime minister would stand in Question Period and say, "I have the name of a female officer who was killed in combat action against the Taliban forces. I am not at liberty to release the name. The next of kin, a husband, is being notified. These are always terrible tragedies. I do not know if this is the first female combat death. It is certainly not a first that we ever want to celebrate...."

Goddard was serving as a forward artillery observer, whose job—
one of the most dangerous in the unit—was to target the Canadian
guns blasting suspected Taliban positions. She and other soldiers from
the 1st Regiment, Royal Canadian Horse Artillery, based in Shilo, Man-
itoba, were forming a ring around the battle area in which Afghan
forces were in close combat with the Taliban fighters. Above, US military jets flew low and pounded the area. About two hundred insur-
gents were involved, fighting with rocket-propelled grenades and
Kalashnikov rifles.

Captain Goddard, one of the few women in the CF to have
achieved that rank, was known as a forceful and secure commander
whose troops were extremely loyal. As her friend Captain Harry Craw-
ford later told the media, "They would do anything for her. The soldiers knew her. They would follow her into hell and back."

It was a tough day to lose a soldier. Earlier that afternoon, the usual
ban on alcohol at the Kandahar base had been lifted, and Canadian soldiers were allowed to have two beers. That night there was a four-hour
concert featuring native stars, including country rocker Michelle Wright.

The plan had been that everyone stay on base. But the plan was
apparently more far-reaching than the officers who led the action, in
which Goddard was killed understood. Or perhaps they understood it
perfectly.

Around six I got to 24 Sussex. It had been thirteen years since I'd been
inside, and nothing much but the artwork seemed to have changed.

The last time here, I'd met Kim Campbell, luxuriating on a couch
with a dozen cushions on it in a second-floor room spectacularly overlooking the rapids in the river. She asked me to be in her cabinet, and
we had tea. It was an otherworldly moment, but then, she was not a
Stephen Harper-like politician.

This time I had been invited for dinner along with some other MPs only because, I presumed, this was Monday and a certain list had popped up on Mrs. Harper's agenda list at the PMO. But it was still appreciated, if only because I knew she read the blog and had been aware of my painfully public falling out with her husband on the appointment of David Emerson and subsequent issues.

As I described it on my blog:

The prime minister's residence is old and rambling and less than perfect, and yet utterly charming. It perches on a high bank overlooking the Ottawa River and these days had been turned into a regular little fortress with RCMP guardhouses and black mechanized driveway barriers that could stop a bus. The grounds are beautiful, but the house is far from being remote from the public. The road, Sussex Drive, is just a couple of hundred feet away, and it is impossible for the occupants to come and go through the front door without being seen. Very Canadian. Inside, it is elegantly comfortable and unpretentious. Fresh flowers are the most opulent detail, and they are everywhere.

The guests this night were Cools, Jim Flaherty, and five members of the finance committee. Laureen Harper was friendly, but perceptively less than she'd been half a year before when she came and campaigned for me in Halton. That night she'd been frank, honest, and compelling. She is, as I have written of her, "no shy and retiring political spouse but—like mine—obviously considers this grand experience to be very much a family affair. She is openly ambitious for him, perceptive and intuitive. She is outspoken. He makes no attempt whatsoever to change that. They are very different people—icebreaker and ice, some would say. It works."

Laureen had told me, "I'm a small town girl, from Turner Valley, Alberta, and I met Stephen at a Reform Party policy convention. So what does that tell ya?" It tells us, of course, that Mrs. Harper, the former Laureen Teskey, is a political animal, just like her husband. Canny, aware, perceptive, she is no decorative spouse, but an integral part of the leadership of the Conservative Party of Canada. She's also a blog addict.

Just before midnight one September night in 2005, when I was campaigning daily for the election yet to be called, she sent me this note:

Hi Garth, my name is Laureen Harper (Stephen is my husband) and I just wanted to say that I have passed on a copy of your blog today for Stephen to read.

Sometimes this job is fun, sometimes it isn't, but the part I hate the most is all the infighting. I wonder sometimes if we conservatives actually spent as much time working the streets (like you are doing) as we did bitching we would win a majority.

Traveling with Stephen this summer we got the same reaction you did. People came up to us all the time to tell Stephen to keep fighting. In fact, we were in New York this weekend for a few days and people were coming up to us in Times Square and talking about the Gomery Inquiry.

Best of luck. Keep up the great work. Remember you are appreciated.

Laureen

This, by the way, is a portion of that blog posting Laureen Harper was responding to, in which I defended her husband against an internal party attack. In it the point is also made that the Conservative Party— my party—is bigger than any one leader. At the time, I believed it.

Here on the street, block by block, event by event, person by person, politics is about establishing respect and trust. If people like you and feel they can put their confidence in you, then the odds are you have their vote. In their hearts, people understand what it is to be a small-c conservative—this is an expression of the core values of moderation, prudence, reasonableness, and compassion. It is what Canadians are all about.

Political hacks, and the media that feed them and feed off them, see politics in a completely different light. They concentrate not on the voters, but on the leaders. Not on communities, but on parties. Not on values, but on policies and theories. So their views are usually myopic and destructive.

I thought of that this morning when I was sent a copy of an open letter from Carol, a Conservative organizer in Etobicoke. It is a three-page dump on Stephen Harper written by a woman who says she helped recruit Belinda Stronach to run for party leader. She wants Harper to resign. If he does not, she asks, "How does that help us convince Mr. and Mrs. Average Canadian that we hear their concerns...?"

Maybe I'm too simple, but it seems to me that once you pick a leader, you support that leader. It also strikes me the leader is but one aspect of a political party and what we all should be doing within that party. The political process is deeper and bigger than one man, regardless of what the media tells you. Leaders come and leaders go, while the people remain.

How do we convince Mr. and Mrs. Average Canadian? You talk to them, Carol.

Fast-forward nine months and the leader, the prime minister, Stephen Harper came into the living room at 24 Sussex, shook hands, and took a straight chair in front of the fireplace, facing the parallel couches, while Laureen sat opposite, at the end of the piano. He attacked a crystal bowl of mixed nuts on the coffee table, which would be all but finished by the time the white-coated chef was ready to serve.

He was forthright, conversational, and engaging. I could not have imagined that three months later his office would be actively encouraging a TV evangelist to scoop my nomination, or that two months after that I'd be publicly expelled from my own party. But here I was, in the man's living room, having been stiffed two bucks by his daughter for some school project, listening to his side of the war in Afghanistan.

Of course, I knew I was just a name on a list of caucus members that the Harpers wanted to grind through—one of the burdens of leadership. Brian Mulroney used to accomplish the same thing, but with breakfasts at 24 Sussex, where five or six MPs would try to pretend they chose each morning from huge platters of fruit, mounds of fresh baking, and eggs Florentine served by waiters with white gloves.

And whereas Mulroney was all cufflinks, starch, Cross pen, and crispness, the Harpers exude a more just-folks, hockey-parents, minivan, suburban Calgary feel. It was casual, but hardly comforting. This man was so in charge, the air crackled with intimidation.

In the Commons a couple of hours earlier, Harper had announced the untimely death of Captain Goddard and heaped praise upon our troops. "There are risks for Afghans, risks for our allies, and as we all know, risks for Canadians," he said. "We know this because we had again today a combat fatality. These risks, as tragic as they are, and these losses, as tragic as they are, are not unique to this time and this place. There were risks when Canada went to the Balkans, to Cyprus, or during the Suez crisis, and of course, in Korea and two world wars.

"Canadians accept risks when those risks are in the service of a greater good. We honour those who take risks and make the ultimate sacrifice by staying the course and supporting their mission." The Commons would reward the prime minister with a narrow vote to extend the Afghan mission until early 2009, cost unknown.

But while the troops had the prime minister's support, and while the death of Nichola Goddard was regrettable and unfortunate, it also ignited Stephen Harper. Mrs. Harper made a comment about the terrible things that had just happened, when her husband looked up and replied, "They were supposed to stay on the goddamned base. And now, this . . ."

The room froze. Unexpected.

A soldier had died. A young, female soldier. The first. But in that moment it left Mr. Harper unable to convey anything but anger.

Others know Stephen Harper far better than I and undoubtedly have a different opinion of the man. Some media types have painted an extremely flattering view of an aggressive, cocksure, smart guy who will take Canada to new levels. Others say the Harper they knew as an opposition politician in their dining rooms making small talk turned out to be a manipulator who now won't acknowledge them in the hallway.

Certainly my dealings with him have been difficult. He treated me with contempt, disdain, derision, and a whiff of disgust. His opinion of me was clearly formed before we ever spoke, and he was sticking with it. As a result, it all turned out badly. In a political sense there was nothing more Stephen Harper could possibly have done to me other than kick me out of the Conservative Party, strip away the nomination I'd won, ban me from ever again representing the party I'd grown up in, take away my useful work in the House of Commons, and dishonour me with the legacy of being an untrustworthy colleague and a caucus cheat.

It could be an ignoble end for a guy who got back into politics to do the ethical thing. Or maybe I was just a fool. Perhaps it was my own fault for not knowing or understanding Stephen Harper or his brand of politics. As Harper himself told me, being a politician and a journalist are mutually exclusive. Journalists think they have to tell the truth. Politicians know better.

CHAPTER SEVEN

"I have become an addict."

—Janine Kreiber, wife of Stéphane Dion

When Turner got kicked out of the Conservative party caucus, it was ultimately <u>his blogging that was to blame</u>. Now, his blogging has gotten him into trouble again.... He's already dug himself out of the government caucus, into opposition, into the Opposition Leader's bad books, and god only knows where next.

—Blogger "Nexus of Assholery," 02 07 08

Who the hell does Garth Turner think he is, to use his blog to launch a personal attack on me?

—Jennifer Wright, Green Shift Inc. founder, in announcing an $8.5-million suit against the Liberal Party of Canada, 2008

STÉPHANE DION WAS ON THE LINE. PISSED.

Late Thursday afternoon in the summer of 2008, and he was in Calgary, trying to talk Albertans into the wisdom of a carbon tax. It was not going well, and he'd just been besieged with media wanting to know about Garth Turner and his blog.

"You have caused a lot of trouble," the Liberal leader told me. "This is now on the front page of *La Presse*. The ADQ has made negative comments about you, and this is very bad. You said that separatists are lazy, but you cannot do that." He paused. I was silent. "You will write on your blog that you are sorry. . . ."

In the end, I'd do no such thing. Being non-digital, Dion did not understand that words posted on a site can never be sucked back, erased, or hidden so they fade from public memory like a distant speech. They live on in a thousand links, in the screen captures of close observers or computer caches and server backups. Yet I could understand the anguish Dion was going through. It personified the clash between old and new, between the mainstream media agenda and digital politics, between reacting to the words of other politicians and communicating with the people themselves.

Getting off the plane from Ottawa, he'd first heard of a blog posting I'd made about his trip to Alberta when his assistant, Gianluca Cairo, handed him his BlackBerry (Dion doesn't carry one), at the same time the media calls were coming in. On the little screen was one sentence from the blog posted the previous night—words now lighting a fire in two provinces.

Ironically, my post had been in uncritical defence of the guy and his challenge to Stephen Harper for a debate on climate change strategies, in the wake of his controversial carbon tax plan launch. Ever the retail politician, Harper had said simply, standing purposefully on Saskatchewan soil, that the Dion Green Shift plan "would screw everybody in the country." Now Dion was trying to recover with a foray into red meat and oil territory where Liberals and taxes are always linked, always hated.

As the Liberal leader was in the air, winging west, I posted this:

Rather than saying the Green Shift will "screw everybody across the country," and have Jason Kenney spew lines about the ancient National Energy Program, this would be a chance for both leaders to clearly articulate their opposing views. Mr. Harper's plan, called "Turning the Corner," has stated that it will cause energy prices for consumers to rise, but without an income tax reduction to offset it. The Conservative plan is based on intensity, while the Liberal plan is a tax on every ton of carbon that industry emits. Conservatives have endorsed the concept of cap and trade, but just not now. The Libs are not far off that position. The government's plan would have results in 2020, while the Liberal plan would affect carbon dumping almost immediately.

Most dramatically, the Conservatives say the Liberal plan would cost consumers, hobble the economy, and be unfair to the West. The Libs say the Con plan is a sham since it will have almost no environmental impact, end up making all energy more expensive, do nothing to help consumers cope or assist businesses to go green.

Meanwhile Canadians are freaked out about gas prices, worried about economic slowdown, and think governments are doing nothing about the future of the planet. In other words, what would be better to crystallize positions and help us all understand the problem and the solutions, than a debate?

But, sadly, ain't gonna happen. The prime minister will not play. This is either because (a) he knows he will lose because his plan sucks, or (b) he does not want to give the leader of the opposition equal footing with Himself, or (c) too many pancakes will die, or (d) he feels sorry for the skinny guy, or (e) it's just a lot easier to say "this will screw everybody."

As for Dion, he will move from Calgary to Edmonton, where he's to have an open Town Hall meeting on his climate change plan. You might not agree with everything the man says, but you have to admire this about him. He stood up once to the self-aggrandizing, hostile, me-first, greedy, macho, selfish, and balkanizing separatist losers in Quebec. I guess he can do it again in Alberta.

Not that there are any similarities.

It took but hours for the storm to roll in. Quebec media latched onto the words first, ignoring the fact I had referenced Dion's Clarity Act initiative following the 1995 referendum, and instead morphing my "separatist losers" into a description of today's sovereignists. Reaction was immediate. Action démocratique du Québec leader Mario Dumont said he was "bowled over" by my words. "Mr. Turner presents Stéphane Dion as a man of courage for standing up to Quebeckers who are described in horrible terms. The Liberal leader must impose sanctions for these shocking comments which are insulting to all Quebeckers."

Federal NDP leader Jack Layton, keen on winning more seats in Quebec and more votes from soft nationalists (as was Dion), said of me, "This kind of contempt has no place in politics." And Conservative environment minister John Baird, on his way to the G8 Summit in Japan, said my words were "outrageous and regrettable.

"These comments are mean-spirited, nasty, divisive and frankly don't reflect well on someone who's a member of Stéphane Dion's inner team." The Conservatives, too, were targeting sovereignist support, a key reason for Stephen Harper's 2007 initiative in having the Quebecois declared a "nation" by Parliament.

Soon my email inbox was clogged with vicious notes, mostly in French, from pro-independence Quebeckers whose most effective English was "Fuck you Turner." The blog received four hundred comments in a few hours, and I deleted hundreds more too graphic to publish. By the time Dion called, I was being widely accused of racism, as if those who wanted out of Canada's political union were members of a special gene pool.

In Alberta, the reaction was as intense. *National Post* columnist Lorne Gunter said that my words suggested "those in the West who oppose his party's new Green Shift carbon tax scheme are un-Canadian.

"This is an old Liberal trick," the old Reformer wrote. "Equate the national interest with Liberal policies, then question the loyalty of anyone who disagrees."

And the front page of the *Calgary Herald* carried a story on the same day as the start of the Stampede headlined, "Grit's blog slurs Alberta." In Quebec, my rip into 1995 separatists had been turned into an attack on the 3.5 million people polls showed were sovereignists today. In Alberta it was simpler—Garth Turner was attacking everyone. Libs against the oilpatch. NEP II. The reincarnation of Pierre Trudeau. The flaccid East versus the rising West.

Dion was cornered. "He retracted and it's not something we want to do," he told reporters on the Stampede grounds, wearing a Stetson, blue checked shirt, brown cowboy boots, and blue jeans with worn knees. "We want to have a respectful debate. Garth explained himself and needed to."

Without a doubt, Dumont, Layton, Baird, or Dion had not read my blog posting when they commented on it. The past tense of the Quebec separatist losers was gone. So was the link between secessionists in the East with those in the West. But that was hardly the issue, since Dion was reacting to other politicians who were reacting to reporters who had cherry-picked ugly-sounding words from an MP's blog. I'd handed Dion's opponents, all lobbying to contain his support in Quebec and the West, a fine stick to beat him with.

The next day, the *Calgary Herald* carried this editorial, which was reprinted the morning after in the *Saskatoon Star Phoenix* and the *Edmonton Journal*:

> Once a Tory, now a Liberal MP, Garth Turner used his blog last week to call Albertans "a bunch of self-aggrandizing, hostile, me-first, greedy, macho, selfish and balkanizing separatist losers ... just like the separatists in Quebec."
>
> We admire his directness. No point crafting innuendoes when a simple insult will do. Now, Albertans know where they

stand with Garth. (So do Quebeckers.) That's more than we can say for his boss, Stéphane Dion, who said the party was seeking a more respectful debate than Turner was offering. But, of course, the debate is over a so-called green plan that appears to be a way of siphoning money out of the West for social programs in the East. That's hostile, too.

The obvious explanation is that it's the same old thing: The Liberals have so little to lose in the West, they might as well be hostile if it helps them gather votes in the East. What else is new? It keeps happening, from the NEP, to Jean Chretien's "tough love" speech, in which he asserted his preference for doing business with easterners, to his lectures about values, as though ours were inferior to those conceived in central Canada, and the consistent Liberal strategy toward the West of acting first, and consulting later. The whole Kyoto Protocol fiasco is a case in point.

And so on. No wonder the Reform Party got to first base yelling, "The West wants in." The truth is, there's a part of central Canada that just doesn't seem to like what the West stands for. It could be envy, it might also be anxiety that Alberta's star is rising as theirs is falling. It could be tribalism that in Ontario requires a pickup-driving out-group to despise in order to elevate one's own self-esteem. Never mind that Ontario builds the trucks, or that the people buying them produce oil everybody uses.

Whatever it is, loathing Alberta seems to be fun and easy. Would it make a difference if we apologized for that bumper sticker about letting them freeze in the dark? Probably not.

After all, how does one engage with a blogger who's a bit "self-aggrandizing, hostile, me-first," himself—or the leader who doesn't shut him up?

Interestingly enough, the editorial writer wasn't content to use my exact words about Albertans, but added to them, "just like the separatists in Quebec." When I asked editorial page editor Licia Corbella about it in an email, she replied, "I will look into this. I'm very surprised that a quote would get changed on purpose. Knowing the person who wrote it, I am certain it was inadvertent." But, as far as readers were concerned, I was a blogger who just needed to be shut down.

As it turned out, Corbella called me a day later with an explanation. Her call, I thought, was worthy blogging about, since the *Herald* was still reprinting my out-of-context quote daily:

> You may recall that recently I got my tail feathers caught in the wringer, which almost never happens. In this instance I blogged about Stéphane Dion's recent trip to Alberta and scrawled a few choice words about separatists, of the Quebec and Western varieties. As a result, two provinces burst into flames and my leader chewed me out.
>
> Anyway, the *Calgary Herald* played a big role by writing an editorial called "The gall of Garth" which began, "Once a Tory, now a Liberal MP, Garth Turner used his blog last week to call Albertans 'a bunch of self-aggrandizing, hostile, me-first, greedy, macho, selfish and balkanizing separatist losers . . . just like the separatists in Quebec.'

In response, I wrote this letter:

> Because I know the *Herald* likes to be accurate, please note the quote you attributed to me in your editorial is incorrect. In fact, I wrote this on my blog (the words are still there) in reference to Stéphane Dion: "He stood up once to the self-aggrandizing, hostile, me-first, greedy, macho, selfish and balkanizing separatist losers in Quebec. I guess he can do it again in Alberta."
>
> The difference? My sentence referred to Quebec separatists following the 1995 referendum. The clear inference was that Dion

could do the same to Westerners who like to talk secession. The reference was not to all Albertans. Worse, the Calgary Herald actually made up part of this quote—"just like the separatists in Quebec."

Yeah, I know it helped make your case that "Albertans know where they stand with Garth." But it wasn't true. Almost all Albertans are proud Canadians who share my faith in a great future together. Some are losers who threaten Easterners. The best way forward is to be honest and open with each other, and a great newspaper can lead the way.

I just wanted you to know what really happened, in case you believe the Alberta media—and the Calgary Herald in particular—are out to throw gas on this story of East-West, Liberal-Conservative, Green Shift-NEP II tension. Frankly, I was a little worried about yellow journalism myself until the editorial page editor of the Herald called me, and we had a good, long chat.

Seems the guy who wrote that editorial was having a bad day. It was his anniversary, plus he had another column to write, plus the Herald had some computer problems which prevented him in his celebratory rush from checking my original words. So, he kinda fudged it, and picked what he thought was my quote from a reader's email.

"It was," she told me, "a bizarre event. And believe me, it was not intentional." And I did believe her.

The editorial writer had a rushed day and was worried about his anniversary. I had my intestines handed to me. I mean, let's put this in perspective.

Ten minutes after those words appeared on the blog, at 10 p.m. on a Friday night in July, I received this email: "I wasn't aware that you were going to post the contents of my private telephone conversation with you on your blog," Corbella wrote. "Had I known that, I would not have conversed with you."

So while it was an honest mistake to alter a politician's words in a way that inflamed public opinion, diminished his capital, and damaged his colleagues, it was out of bounds to publish the reason behind that mistake? Hardly. What had Licia's knickers in a knot was that a blog had uncovered a small failure of the mainstream media, and the new media was exposing the old. Getting a message out to the people had been the private preserve of her profession for generations. But no more. A blogger was putting a journalist under the scope. She didn't like it one bit.

Days later, the issue was still alive, as political opponents sought to capitalize on a single sentence in a blog posting, with disregard for the original meaning. In an article trashing Stéphane Dion's Green Shift initiative, the Conservative Party website said it was deplorable "that Dion's senior communications advisor, Garth Turner, would respond to legitimate criticisms of the Dion Tax Trick by labelling ordinary people as, 'self-aggrandizing, hostile, me-first, greedy, macho, selfish and balkanizing separatist losers.'"

So, the evolution was complete. From a swipe at Quebec separatists of 1995 and Western secessionists of today, my words had evolved into a condemnation of everyone in Quebec who's a sovereignist, then to a slight against an entire race (not sure which one), then to an insult to Albertans, then to a blanket Eastern slur on Westerners, to an attack on my "political opponents," and finally a deplorable comment on "ordinary people."

Of course, this little incident would never have happened without that blog. I hadn't given a widely covered speech on the carbon tax, or been asked by Radio-Canada, RDI, or *La Presse* for my views on the Quebec pro-independence movement. I was two thousand miles away from Calgary at the time, and hadn't spoken to Dion in the two weeks since we launched his carbon tax plan. In fact, I had not spoken to any reporter or stepped in front of any camera. But suddenly I was getting more attention than the leader. On CTV's cable news network that weekend, an interview I gave rebelliously leaning against my new motorcycle was the lead item on newscasts repeated every half hour. Dion's trip to Calgary was second. In the days following I was suddenly in media demand across the country, while the Liberal leader's office struggled to get reporters to attend a Town Hall meeting in Edmonton.

But it wasn't about me. It was about the persona of me. The digital me. And that had been created by the blog. In fact, it was the blog.

This should show every leader, every party, the growing influence and reach—wanted or not—of digital politics. It also highlights the inevitable and often destructive clash between the old and new media. An interactive and voter-based blog is inherently different than top-down traditional media. Instead of being a vehicle in which reporters and columnists digest and interpret the news, it is the news. That's what made it such a powerful tool in the hands of Barack Obama. It's why this is probably the future of politics.

But until a party leader or minister has the courage and confidence to interact digitally with voters, or comment-driven blogs are the expected norm for every elected MP, the clash will continue. The mainstream media saw the country's first blogging MP as a rich source of protein, and seized upon his words with unreasonable enthusiasm. So, why doesn't a leader harness this, not only to influence the media agenda, but to directly communicate with an increasingly online nation? What is the political establishment afraid of? Why was my blogging so dreaded within the Conservative Party that it played a pivotal role in my ouster?

Because, of course, it's as insanely dangerous as it is gloriously democratic.

✧

Three years of running a blog and everything has changed in terms of his exposure. Don't be surprised people, if there are a number of other individuals that follow the examples set here and now because this very blog of which words we read are setting a precedent as we speak and it has power in terms of its influences on professors, journalists, voters, MPs, policy makers, business, make no mistake. I'm not saying that most MPs can walk in Garth's footsteps because they just don't have the same experience/background. One has to have pure writing skills and have a background in publishing/editing to really make it fly and that makes Garth a one of a kind so to speak but look at the effect this blog is having on Canadian politics! I see other MPs following this footstep down the road and candidates, if they are wise and want exposure to who they are as people and what they have to offer, the best way is with a daily blog online and I can't help but think that there will be takers. I can see, actually, pure bloggers becoming candidates themselves just as journalists have so successfully in the past.

—Anonymous blog comment, on garth.ca, 12 July, 2008, 22:47

Garth Turner is the gift that keeps on giving.

—The Grumpy Voter (Conservative blogger), August 2008

Blogging removes the filters which have always existed between politicians and voters. Gone are the media interpreters, the reporters, and columnists who might be influenced. Gone are the Prime Minister's Office and Office of the Leader of the Opposition (OLO) spin doctors, chiefs of staff, communications directors, or front-line assistants in MPs' offices who can massage, augment, and polish a message. Most of all, gone is deniability, and the refuge of being misquoted, interpreted wrongly, or merely screwed over by a hostile or incompetent journalist. A blogging politician cannot suck back damaging words or a misplaced thought. The digital footprint is indelible. It's permanent.

In fact, the very culture of digital communications prevents that. If you said it once, it exists forever. Old postings cannot be deleted without a valid reason, and changing your mind isn't one of them. Comments made a month or a year or a decade ago are dragged up in the ever-widening nets of Google to be as fresh a catch as the day they were made. There's no going back, only going forward. You can clarify, and explain. Never retract. The sequence of time is lost with digital, web-based communications, since past actions and words are glued on to those from yesterday. Riddled with errors or not, its entries secretly edited by supporters or foes to enhance or diminish a reputation, Wikipedia has become an online shrine of knowledge for those who want instant research. Suddenly opponents and critics who seek to blow you up can mine an inexhaustible seam of information, especially if you happen to add a thousand fresh words a day on a blog.

The shattering of this traditional wall between the people and those who represent them is an unprecedented and positive breakthrough in the way we're governed. It allows not only instant access to politicians, but an open forum in which citizens can praise, trash, or influence them. Unlike a Town Hall meeting, a blog forum is as close as the home computer, always on and blessedly anonymous. Unlike with door-knocking, which is intrusive and therefore usually ineffective, digital constituents can have a one-on-one encounter with the person they elected, on their own terms, not dripping wet out of the shower or pulled away from feeding the dog. And for the elected person, this is a way of reaching out daily to dozens, hundreds or—as I have experienced—hundreds of thousands of people together, and regardless of your location or schedule.

When elected again in January 2006, I was high on the narcotic of digital democracy. Sitting in a downscale neighbourhood restaurant in mid-Toronto, I mapped out with brilliant webmaster William Stratas a strategy for blogging, live and on-demand webcasting, and an interactive website that would break new ground in allowing citizens access to the federal political system. I hoped, and naively believed, that we were creating a template for my new caucus, whose members would embrace this as the obvious new dawn of political responsiveness.

In the coming weeks I bought a mess of video and used television broadcast equipment at my own expense, built a webcasting facility and studio in my Ottawa office, and forged a unique data pipeline agreement with an intrigued House of Commons. I hired staff that could shoot, edit, and broadcast as well as perform basic Hill tasks, then launched a weekly, hour-long webcast branded as MPtv.

Over the next months I would load the website with hundreds of hours of on-demand original video content, made up mostly of candid on-location interviews with MPs from all parties, asking them why they were in Ottawa, what they hoped to accomplish during their time, and how they'd make the country better. Not only did this give viewers a unique window into the House of Commons, and backbench MPs exposure most of them never got from the mainstream media, but it allowed me to drift every day back and forth across the deep partisan divide that keeps Conservatives from ever talking to Liberals, NDP, or separatist deputies from Quebec.

Little did I understand at first how that simple act of standing in the foyer of the House, interviewing opposition MPs under my battered, used TV lights and wearing obsolete hard-wired mics while my staff member held the camera, amid the swirl of the post-QP scrum, would seal my fate with the Harper team. (This would be revealed fully after I was ousted, and Conservatives used the House of Commons security staff to harass, impede, and eventually shut down my MPtv effort in early 2008.)

Meanwhile I made the effort to blog daily, but not in the form of a personal online diary. Instead, I put my journalist's training to use in writing and posting a column with a current affairs purpose to it, with adequate research and as much insider insight as possible. As a result,

website traffic grew steadily, quickly, and commensurate with the negative impact digital democracy was having on my own political career.

When Dick Harris, chair of the BC Conservative caucus, unexpectedly accused me in national caucus one Wednesday morning of
running MPtv as a commercial, for-profit operation, and, worse, giving a subversive forum to opposition MPs, it was clearer what the future
would hold: conflict. But with an uneasy Stephen Harper watching, I
stood defiantly, went to the podium normally reserved for him, and
responded, saying my colleagues had nothing to fear from me, or from
the new ideas or technology I was bringing into their midst.

But they did. Intuitively and intensely. From that morning on,
cabinet ministers and virtually all Conservative MPs declined repeated
invitations from my office to be interviewed. The zenith of suspicion
and hostility was reached on the day I've already mentioned, when
Green Party leader Elizabeth May and I stood in the foyer to tape an
episode for broadcast on garth.ca. I asked her what she wanted and
expected out of the Harper green plan, about to be announced. By the
time that plan was made public, not too many hours later, I would be
an independent.

Several years after sitting in the Toronto restaurant, mapping the
path to an interactive and online Parliament accessible by all, truly
responsive, and accountable to everyone, I'm convinced of its inevitability. While blogging politicians are a rarity, and webcasting ones
virtually unknown, surely every election in the future will bring new
people who understand the power of being digital. They'll think nothing of communicating by blog, video, and email on a number of platforms and devices. They'll demand the House of Commons put an end
to the slaughter of entire forests to send out "householders" and "ten
percenters," which end up in the blue boxes of millions of Canadians.
Online chats, interactive sites, MP forums and discussion boards,
real-time webcasting, and remote public meetings will be common-
place. And politicians who embrace the new technologies, welcoming

public input as a core part of their jobs, will never again feel feared, ostracized, shunned, or ultimately rejected by their colleagues, parties, or leaders.

But today, non-digital politicians like Harper and, before his post-election resignation, Dion struggle in a landscape of changing voter expectations. When the Liberal leader asked me not only to apologize, but expunge my Quebec/West separatist statement, he fully expected it to be erased. When it was not, my troubles only deepened. But Dion was playing by an old set of rules, in which past statements are replaced by new ones as simply as typing over them. Of course, Stephen Harper shares this view, product of a political culture in which search engines and YouTube didn't really matter and past policies can stay in the past. If he changed his mind on income trusts, fixing capital gains taxes, or supporting Quebec nationalism, so what? Voters are just people with busy lives. They'll get over it.

But it's too late.

✧

Digital politics is unstoppable.

My blog has made it into the official residences in Ottawa at 24 Sussex and Stornoway. It was not read by Stephen Harper or Stéphane Dion, but rather by their wives.

I knew this from Laureen Harper's emails to me (which stopped abruptly with my ouster from her husband's caucus) and from the frequent comments of Dion's spouse, Janine Kreiber. Both have told me they've taken columns and comments from there and drawn them to their husbands' attention.

"I must tell you," Janine confided in me during the spring of 2008, "that I have become an addict."

Also feeding a new blog habit is the OLO, as well as the PMO, where the prime minister's staff directs the activities of ministers and the Conservative Party. Senior Dion policy advisors as well as the chief of staff made no secret of monitoring the blog daily, while on the floor of the House of Commons words from my site were used as weapons against me by, among others, Finance Minister Jim Flaherty, House Leader Peter van Loan, and Environment Minister John Baird. Daily QP ministerial briefing books contain yellow pages on which were quoted phrases and sentences from the blog that could be quickly grabbed as cannon fodder in the Commons war.

Perhaps nowhere is the digital skirmish more intense than on the official governing party website, conservative.ca, devoted to an all-out attack on everything Liberal. Once again, the inherent risk of daily blogging is made obvious there.

Like the time I supposedly accused Canadian soldiers of murdering Afghan civilians.

That episode began with a talk I gave to religious leaders in my riding of Halton, alluding to Canada's leapfrogging military spending at a time when funds for a local youth shelter were lacking. A tape of that event revealed that I said, "Our country is spending $150,000 on every artillery shell that we're shooting in Afghanistan. Those artillery shells have GPS—they've got computers in the tips of them. And those computers fulfill no function but to guide that shell from our Canadian Army howitzers into villages to kill people." The people were ones I'd just spoken about—Taliban insurgents.

But a local reporter thought she heard this: "We don't have funding for youth centres but we do have $150,000 for every shell bought for the sole purpose of destroying a village in Afghanistan."

Based on her newspaper report, and the immediate foaming reaction of Conservative bloggers, the CPC site stated categorically that I was accusing our troops of murder. "In a time when Canadians should be rallying behind our men and women in uniform, it is ignorant and outrageous for an opportunistic Opposition MP to instead accuse them of targeting and killing civilians," it said.

So what started in an inconsequential community newspaper in a story written by a reporter who erred was broadcast by partisan blogs, then the *National Post*, then embellished and finally fictionalized by the national Conservative website. Where Stephen Harper's troops could not finish off my career in real life, they sought to do so digitally.

But this only illustrates how badly Canadian political parties have adapted to the new technologies. In order to gain eyeballs, and influence, in a competitive online world, news-oriented political sites have to maintain basic credibility. Even the most partisan of bloggers, like Stephen Taylor (Con) or Jason Cherniak (Lib) have learned they must include references to source material and do actual research in order to carve out a corner of the blogosphere. The standards are raised daily, as viewers eschew daily newspapers and move to news aggregators like Bourque or National Newswatch, then on to sites of opinion and commentary. As they migrate, they expect basic principles of journalism to apply. Successful blogs can no longer be mindless rants, personal diaries, or unsourced spews. They also must carry fresh material as often as possible and, to actually matter, allow reader interaction.

In that context, both Liberals and Conservatives fail the test, despite having substantial resources to throw at their party's crucial online presence. Uber-partisan, badly written and researched, dominated by adolescent Photoshop illustrations of Stéphane Dion, conservative.ca fell far short of the standard being set in the United States. Meanwhile liberal.ca was static, chronically out of date, and visually tepid. Both sites have thus far been afraid of opening up the floodgates of public comment, abandoning a valuable opportunity to kindle debate and involve hundreds of thousands of jaded voters.

The Dion forces made the classic mistake of creating a website—which initially was overwhelmed with traffic—and then gave visitors no reason to return. My simplistic suggestion during the design phase to have an interactive blog was accepted, and a party staffer identified to write it, but the feature never materialized, As a result, the number of eyeballs crested in the first few days, then fell. An opportunity wasted, with just the lawsuit lingering.

Well-meaning and extremely experienced politically, Dion's OLO operatives nonetheless dropped the ball on the carbon tax launch precisely because they underestimated the impact of digital communications.

While there was talk of harnessing the joint power of progressive bloggers, collectively known as Liblogs, for the national launch, it never happened. In contrast, blogging Tories as a group jumped on "Dion's tax on everything," and invested huge amounts of time effectively trashing it.

The expectation of a new, bold, green, web-centric initiative was dashed in days by the launch of a static site seemingly more interested in raising money for the party than helping the environment. Given that the Liberals' plan would appeal most immediately to younger, enviro-conscious voters—the same demographic heavily populating blogs and green websites—this was a fault.

Measurement of Dion's success in selling the plan in the critical summer months following the June launch was done in the traditional way—by monitoring press clippings, while ignoring web-based comment. This gave the OLO strategists a misleading and overly optimistic assessment of the public perception, and led to missteps in planning the leader's tour and positioning and ultimate electoral failure. Leading national newspaper columnists gave the plan a grudging chance, while the buzz in Tim's was something different.

For unknown reasons, Dion refused to order his almost one hundred national caucus members to utilize their office resources to pump the plan. While some attempt was made to provide MPs with mail-out flyers and newsletters, none materialized to co-ordinate a nationwide email blast to constituents and party supporters. In contrast, the Conservative Party stuffed the email inboxes of more than 2.7 million people with Dion's tax-on-everything messages and successful fundraising solicitations.

Did this spell disaster for Stéphane Dion, the Green Shift, or the financially precarious Liberals? Or merely complicate the repositioning of the Liberal leader as a kamikaze risk-taking, non-traditional, political visionary?

In that, we shared. And we both tasted defeat.

When the dust settled from the January 23, 2006, election, there were three MPs writing blogs, all of them Conservatives. Monte Solberg ceased his when appointed to Stephen Harper's cabinet in February of that year. Alberta MP David Anderson gave up his web log in November 2007, a month after I was thrown out of the national Conservative caucus for blogging. Consequently, I was only one to remain.

Since that election, just two other blogging MPs have tried their hand at it. St. Catharines Conservative Rick Dykstra, the one who tried to link me to that murderous Harper joke, keeps an online diary, but the administrator has disabled public write access to it. London North Centre Liberal Glen Pearson started his blog in the spring of 2008, and does allow public comments. Neither Dykstra nor Pearson blog daily, but they are to be lauded for their efforts.

Meanwhile, as I write this, there are over 200,000 comments sitting on my site. Daily expectations are for between one hundred and four hundred new comments, and my webmaster tells me monthly hits are consistently over two million. And while web traffic stats are notoriously unreliable, the influence of the blog on national political life—which is all that really matters—is perhaps easier to gauge. Most members of the parliamentary press gallery tell me they read it daily and that alone makes it influential. It is not unusual at all to see myself quoted in news stories by reporters who never needed to call, since my thoughts were available online.

As I have detailed, the blog both saved me from political ruin, and caused it. There was no doubt in my mind that Stephen Harper would have ejected me sooner from his caucus, in those forty-eight hours after he announced his first cabinet, had I not turned the blog into an instrument of defence, and crossed the line from web presence to op-ed page in dailies across the country. I've also no doubt the Charles McVety forces of the righteous Right would have scooped my Conservative nomination in Halton in the summer of 2006, had I not used the blog to raise national awareness, cast a bright light on their tactics, enrage those who saw it as a hijacking of the democratic process, raise money, and engender critical new local support. By the same token, the blog dumped more than 1.2 million of my words—enough to fill twenty books—into the public domain, 24/7, where they could be picked apart, dissected, bent, and used to define me, in the example of Alberta and Quebec comments above, as a racist, anti-francophone, lazy, Eastern, elitist Liberal Western-hating Toronto MP loser.

So being a digital politician brings both opportunity and danger. But how is that so different than the advent of dailies or radio or television as instruments of national communication? Every interview granted is subject to interpretation by a reporter with his or her own biases. Every clip can be shortened and juxtaposed. Every time a politician opens his or her lips, job security runs screaming in the opposite direction.

And this, ironically, is why blogging is an undeniably superior way of influencing public life. Words may be taken out of context, but they can't be overwritten. More importantly, there is direct contact between the elected and the electors. No matter how distorted your message may be as it struggles through the mainstream media filter, a blogger's original words, as read by the online audience, remain intact. This is the future. So long as you have an audience. And leaders need that.

Marjory LeBreton sat on that little stool of Mike Duffy's a few hours after my career as a Conservative MP had ended, and blamed the blog. Brian Mulroney's former assistant, now a Stephen Harper insider, she closely followed the caucus talking points on Garth Turner that had just been issued by the Conservative Research Group. Colleagues felt they could not discuss things, she told Duffy, "without having it appear on his blog, and therefore in the media." This was consistent with what caucus chair Rahim Jaffer had said when making the announcement. As CTV reported, "He said the suspension was due in part to Turner's blog, which he often uses as a soapbox to make his opinions known."

The television network also reported that "the party had been warning Turner since the summer to stop with the injudicious blogging." It was untrue, but effective at the time, as was the immediate PMO spin that Garth Turner was just pissed because he'd been passed over for a cabinet appointment.

In retrospect, there were many reasons that may have justified Stephen Harper's momentous decision in a minority Parliament to throw one of his too-few MPs overboard. My unrepentant insubordination on the David Emerson and Michael Fortier appointments could have sufficed. My defiance on the issues of same-sex marriage, gun control, or the costly and questionable evacuation from Lebanon could have done it. There was my very public campaign to allow pension-splitting and family income-splitting, complete with a Parliament Hill conference, despite the finance minister's public censure. And my urging of a strong, unequivocal environmental plan, when the Harper cabinet had no intention of writing one, was a potential career-ender.

After all, as I said, Jim Flaherty had stood up in the fateful caucus which finished me off, and found it necessary to tell the room, "Garth Turner is not running an alternative government."

No, I was just a backbencher. With a blog.

Most heinous, though (and ironic for Marjory as she yakked to Duffy about it all), was my openness with the media, and the way the blog had turned into a source of material on the workings of a government that valued secrecy above all. At the end of my days as a Harper team member, it was information that brought me down. That this would happen in the information age, when an online nation had the collective wisdom of humanity at its fingertips, when Google was worth far more on stock markets than General Motors, was telling. Stephen Harper and his political army stood on the ramparts, bravely fighting for a lost time when politicians knew better than the people, when elected officials replaced the electors instead of representing them and decisions were taken quickly, strongly, and quietly without consultation or explanation.

Thus, for example, an election commitment that "a Conservative government will stand for certainty for seniors and never allow raids on seniors' nest eggs by changing investment rules," became a 31 percent tax on income trusts and lost billions in private savings ten months later, announced without notice. A lifelong commitment by Stephen Harper to treat all Canadians equally became, once he was in power, the recognition of one group of citizens as "a nation." And a decision to lower borrowing standards for residential real estate, turning a bull housing market into a dangerous bubble, was reversed one day in the summer of 2008, again without notice, and unwisely as the economy was rapidly deflating.

From landmark changes in the country's immigration policy to unexpectedly raising income tax rates in its first budget, before wildly and unpredictably dropping them a year later, the Harper government preferred to take its decisions in a paternalistic, father-knows-best, no-explanation fashion behind the now heavily guarded doors of the cabinet room. It was a style of government familiar and expected in previous generations, but increasingly at odds with the one now turning from newspapers to news aggregators, from call-in radio to online chats and from trust to skepticism. In a time when hundreds of thousands were surfing blogs and tuning out the corporate media, Harper's spin, control, and opaque style were out of step. And within his very caucus, Garth Turner was a digital Trojan horse.

So in the end, it was not defiance nor insubordination nor policy differences that the prime minister decided would be fatal. It was blogging. My posted words may have been uncomfortable or challenging to the new Conservative government, but it was the digital identity itself, the openness and unpredictability that was simply too much to bear. Stephen Harper is all about management and containment. A blogging MP with a national audience, free-wheeling interactive website, a hundred thousand published and unfiltered comments from Canadian voters, and a penchant for webcasting people of every political stripe was definitely out of control.

Such an MP may be seen as a serious challenge to political parties, and to leaders, but that's simplistic and vain. It's the information technology that has lit the fuse in Ottawa.

Once a person's elected, leaders have demanded a switch in allegiance, from the people to the political organization. Unlike in the American Congress, when politicians often carry a party allegiance and yet remain fierce and ferocious lobbyists for their own electoral districts, Canadian MPs are expected to melt quickly and quietly into a caucus that speaks with one voice—the leader's voice. Individuality is discouraged and open discussion is mistaken as divisive debate. Despite the obvious fact that MPs come from regions thousands of miles apart, inhabited by electors with wildly differing needs and views, leaders demand they start representing the party or the government back to the people, instead of the other way around.

This, I found, was taken to an extreme inside the Harper Conservative cult. From the caucus podium, Harper had warned of dire consequences for any MP who questioned program spending cuts, even if they hurt those people a member was in Ottawa to represent and defend. Every week, communications director Sandra Buckler hammered home the message that only disloyal and disobedient team members would speak to reporters without her permission. Even a decision directly devastating for many vulnerable constituents, like the one to reverse course and tax income trusts, was not open for debate within the caucus room and certainly not outside. Inside the Harper team, MPS were actively discouraged from telling the prime minister what their voters wanted, and simply forbidden from telling the people back home anything without approval.

It's hard to imagine this kind of top-down, information-killing leadership can survive indefinitely, or that web-based direct democracy will not soon challenge all the national parties. Perhaps it already is, hidden in declining voter turnout (a record low number of us voted in 2008) and the plunging membership roles of local riding associations. At a time when the new technologies are empowering voters as never before, Canadians are governed by an administration that has stripped their representatives of almost all influence and power. Harper MPS are rarely allowed to vote freely and my experience showed they're not permitted free speech within the party. They're prevented open access to the media and not a single one carries on an open and interactive online dialogue with the people who elected them.

But Stephen Harper, like Stéphane Dion, knows well that direct democracy undermines the authority of a leader, and digital MPS can be a threat. If Canadians feel they can have unfiltered influence on the political process between elections and delegated leadership conventions, then the electorate grows more influential and leaders less so. Party policy conventions with predetermined outcomes can be written off as marketing events. Voters contributing to political blogs and forums find their voices and expect leaders to start listening. Governing gets messy as citizens want in.

So digital democracy is a problem. For leaders, MPS who maintain a pipeline of accountability to the voters are mutinously dividing their loyalties. For Stephen Harper, I personified that. My crime was information, but my potential for mayhem was far worse. The virus of empowerment might spread.

When Stéphane Dion impetuously but heroically announced he'd travel to the United Nations Climate Change conference in Bali, Indonesia, in December 2007, he assumed Canadians would take note and applaud his effort—the only party leader to make the trip. I didn't, and suggested the Liberal leader do something unique. He should blog about it.

It took a series of meetings of the senior communications team, including Dion's chief of staff, to agree the idea had merit, but the caution was palpable. Even though everyone around the table was a BlackBerry addict and spent 90 percent of their waking time online, with all party players communicating by email—even across the table from each other in the OLO's wood-panelled boardroom—the blog was untested and fraught with danger. Dion's words would be unfiltered and spontaneous. Already senior staff cringed at his unscripted media scrums and spent precious time every day rehearsing lines with him before he walked in front of the post-QP cameras. The idea of him pecking away at a laptop, unsupervised, half a world away was terrifying.

A compromise was struck. The blog would go ahead, but written by a staffer who'd travel with the leader. Dion would be briefed on the contents of each posting and—absolutely—there'd be no interactivity, no comments allowed from the public, for fear Conservative trolls would overwhelm.

But putting his name and face on a ghostwritten blog was inconsistent with a man who routinely wrestled with his staff over the words and phrases and even the punctuation of his speeches. While other leaders and leadership hopefuls routinely commissioned journalists to write "their" books, this was a different medium. And it was a different kind of leader. Only weeks later I would spend two hours in his office, sweltering in the early June heat (Dion refused to turn on the energy-sucking air conditioning unit in his gothic window) revising the first Green Shift brochure, which I'd written the weekend before. The Liberal leader insisted on going over every single sentence and, as we began, came to the table with a copy covered with his trademark indecipherable scrawl.

(Where I had written, poetically, that Liberals will leave nobody behind on this journey of hope, Dion interjected, "We cannot say that. We must say, Liberals will include everyone on this journey. To say it in the other way is sounding like George Bush!")

In the end it was a tepid effort. The blog was devoid of passion, insight, or, as it turned out, news content. The media yawned and the Liberal Party obliterated the postings from its website within a few weeks. But the unintended consequences were still impressive—more than $40,000 in unsolicited donations poured into party coffers over the course of a week (a big deal for Libs, believe me) and the number of hits received by liberal.ca ballooned. For a few days Dion turned into a minor cult figure—the first political party leader with his name on a blog. The first who defied being dooced.

However, the experiment was not enough to immediately convince either Dion or his advisors to embrace this channel of direct communications with Canadians. As a result, he risked continuing to allow the opposition to define him, as he had since becoming party leader in the dying days of 2006. Just months later, in March of 2008, when the Liberal leader began to muse in public about the societal benefits of a carbon tax, the thirty-seven-member Conservative communications machine, led by Guy Giorno—who would four months later take over Ian Brodie's key role in charge of Harper's PMO—was ready to pounce. Between the time of Dion's first carbon tax speech, delivered in Vancouver, and the moment of his Green Shift launch on

Parliament Hill in late June, the Harper effort had resulted in stark, clear messaging, radio ads, a dedicated website, viral marketing campaign, postcards, MP mailers, ministerial attacks across the country, yellow-shirted protesters on the streets of Ottawa, and even a talking, animated grease spot.

In response, Dion made the decision to focus on a summer-long, cross-country series of Town Hall meetings, leaving the airwaves barren of paid advertising and the Green Shift website languishing for critical weeks with stale content, providing no reason for anyone to go there twice. It was the classic response of a traditional twentieth-century politician convinced that in-the-flesh personal appearances are the best offensive weapon, and that the mainstream media would convey his message. Back in the OLO, chief Andrew Bevan read the news clippings and concluded it was all working. In Tim's, they wondered what the Libs were smoking. Bevan forgot that Tim's was where the voters were.

In the end, of course, Stéphane Dion's unique, underestimated, boyish refusal to give up doomed him. When contrasted to Stephen Harper's condescension and prime ministerial arrogance, the Liberal leader's muted, dogged minivan odyssey through small-city Canada may have won hearts and respect, one hall at a time—the remarkable result of an undaunted will—but it was no match for a calculated frontal media onslaught.

Finally, in midsummer 2008 he launched a blog of his own. The Liberal website carried the "Leader's notebook," with Dion's face at the top, his signature at the bottom and a staffer's words in the middle. He never did get it.

But then there's Garth. Normally, I would never, ever expect a backbencher to make these sorts of comments; you don't become a Minister by sticking your neck out, and often don't win elections either, especially in a policy-allergic party like the Liberals. He's sometimes (maybe even often?) wrong, but at least you get the sense that he's not bullshitting you about it. Honest and out-spoken. Heh. No wonder Harper tossed him out.

—Blogger, "Shadow of the Hegemon" 24-07-08

Starkly speaking, my tenure as an MP the second time around was a disaster. Once elected, I immediately fell out of favour with my leader, colleagues, and party. Shunned and feared, I was ultimately expelled from my political family. I became what I could never have imagined, an independent member of Parliament, then a Liberal. And yet my relationship with the leader of my new party was more than once strained and stretched to the point of snapping.

Over the course of three short years I turned into one of the most controversial figures in the House of Commons, spawning entire web-sites dedicated to my ridicule and defeat. I'd been the only sitting MP in the country challenged for a party nomination in his own riding. Without ever giving a speech or leaving my laptop, I'd inflamed Que-bec separatists, enraged congregations of Christians across the coun-try, ignited Westerners, and been held up globally as an example of a star-crossed politician.

No cabinet appointment came my way, no critic's role, chairman's gavel, extra pay, staff, prestige, or title. I was a spokesman for nothing, too independent and edgy for a leader to trust, too unsteady and quixotic to be considered loyal. By choosing principle over party, by pledging my allegiance to the people, I'd made my own bed in Ottawa. By all traditional measures of success there, I enjoyed none.

This came in sharp relief to my first tour of duty in Parliament. As a Progressive Conservative MP under Brian Mulroney, then Kim Campbell, I'd been the only rookie member to be given control of a House of Commons standing committee. I was brought immediately into a policy-making role by Finance Minister Michael Wilson, and hosted national conferences on containing the national debt and enshrining property rights in the Canadian constitution, both influencing government action. I'd found enough support to run for national party leader and was subsequently invited into the cabinet and the Privy Council.

The contrast is remarkable, but why?

Age and experience, of course. They bring more clarity to life's journey. I was better able to see through the aggression and impatience of Stephen Harper, better able to understand the hesitancy and principled reticence of Stéphane Dion.

More pivotal, though, was an embrace of populism, direct democracy, and the tools that now enable them. Some will argue that destroyed me.

But I had to try.

In the earliest days of again becoming a federal politician, I was ordered to cease blogging, and go offline. The prime minister was unequivocal. There was a choice with clear outcomes. Thus, Stephen Harper is not to blame for what came next. Doubtless, he'd make the same decision again, as would I.

He sought to stop the inevitable, surely believing he could. He worked in a traditional way to contain a threat. The weapon he resorted to was his most powerful. Shunned, then expelled, my political legitimacy would be stripped away with my party affiliation. It was a definitive and devastating experience.

While parties are central to how we run countries, it is less so each day. The Internet has the power to turn unknowns into leaders and involve citizens whom partisan recruiters, organizers, and militants will never meet. A blog can alter political outcomes, while websites reach millions when media outlets are still editing. Politicians who open digital conversations make the future impossible for those who do not. One or two more federal elections, and the traditionalists will be gone.

Parties may follow. They'll certainly be transformed. Online members will be harder to control, and more responsive to voters. Ridings will melt away in the digital ascent of issues over geography. And if dozens of independents are ever to take their seats in the House of Commons, it will be because of this. Funded, promoted, and elected through web-based campaigns, they will skirt the rules of a political establishment that abhors them.

Experience has convinced me this is what many Canadians want. Parties and leaders who demand unquestioning acceptance of dogmatic positions are doomed. No one, not even a prime minister, can put this back in the bottle.

In the historic Reading Room of Centre Block, where the government caucus meets, the high stone walls are adorned at each end with Art Deco paintings depicting the liberating influence of newspapers. On the south wall stands a beautiful young woman, draped in satin holding a torch, opposite the grizzled operator of a press. Beneath her is inscribed, "The Spirit of the Printed Word."

I have stared up a hundred times. She'd blog.

On the web

Garth Turner invites you to be a part of an ongoing discussion arising out of this book. Or, feel free to talk with him about his book on the troubled future of real estate, *Greater Fool*. Garth's daily blog on the economy, investments, personal finance, real estate and the turbulent times we are in is constantly updated, and fully open for your comments and questions.

Access this valuable resource through either of these web site addresses:

www.garth.ca

www.AfterTheCrash.ca

Through email

To send a comment directly to Garth Turner, use this email address. It will reach him immediately.

garth@garth.ca

In person

In addition to his career in politics, Garth Turner is one of the country's most experienced, exciting and motivating public speakers. He has entertained and educated audiences across North America, and will consider a live appearance for keynote addresses, public or private seminars, client workshops, industry or consumer shows, conventions or community groups. Contact him directly by phone or email:

(416) 346-0086

garth@garth.ca